Praise for

THiNKING CONSCIOUSLY ROCKS!

"Connie Williams has been through the refiner's fire, and now she wants to share with you what came out of her alchemical process. Just as her thinking changes, so too will yours as you read her book."

> —**C. Gordon Peerman, D.Min., author of**
> ***Blessed Relief: What Christians Can Learn from Buddhists about Suffering***

"Connie Williams has delivered a truly personal and touching book, straight from the heart."

> —**Seth Godin, author of *We Are All Weird***

"I urge you to do something special for others and yourself— read "Thinking Consciously Rocks!" The investment of your time will come back multiplied with more personal light, joy, and victory and will illuminate the way for others whom you touch along the way."

> —**Dan Miller, author and life coach, *48 Days to the Work You Love* and *No More Dreaded Mondays***

"The intentionality to grow is the power that radiates from Connie Williams. She helps us understand that we have that same power to live our lives and not just cope with them. Through her story she shows us how she found her way home."

> —**Judy Nebhut, Nashville photographer**
> **www.JudyNebhut.com**

"Connie Williams has created a life changing masterpiece overflowing with pearls of wisdom and deeply moving moments. I could literally feel my Being shift with each passing page. Give yourself the gift of, "Thinking Consciously Rocks," and watch the miracles begin to unfold in your own life."

—Paul Dolman, author
Hitchhiking With Larry David: You Never Know When the Magic Will Happen

THI*N*KING CONSCIOUSLY ROCKS!

CHANGING YOUR LIFE ONE CONSCIOUS THOUGHT AT A TIME

Connie M. Williams

N/\P

Nashville Advertising & Promotions, Inc.

NASHVILLE, TENNESSEE

THiNKING CONSCIOUSLY ROCKS! Changing Your Life
One Conscious Thought at a Time

www.thinkingconsciouslyrocks.com

This book is manufactured in the United States.

Unattributed quotes are by Connie Williams.

Publisher:

Nashville Advertising & Promotions, Inc.
PO Box 291985
Nashville, Tennessee 37229-1985

Bulk Orders:

If you would like to place a bulk order of books for your group
or association please contact the publisher at
nap1994@comcast.net.

Sheila,

Thank you for our journey together

and for helping me heal.

To my family and friends—thank you for your love

and support—you all make my heart smile.

To Dad and Carl

Carl M. Williams, my brother

(1961-1994)

Charles W. Williams, my father

(1933-1994)

"Out beyond ideas of wrong doing
and right doing, there is a field.
I will meet you there."
—*Rumi*

Contents

ADVANCE PRAISE I

FOREWORD XII

CHAPTER 1

FROM MURDER TO MINDFULNESS

Growing Up 2

Wednesday, April 20, 1994 4

The Deceased Was Named Williams........... 5

The Detectives Arrive 6

The Force That Drove Me to Write This Book 7

The Growing Up Years............. 8

Wanting More 9

CHAPTER 2

THE SAME BUT DIFFERENT..........15

New Influences 18

The Same but Different............ 21

CHAPTER 3

CHANGING OUR THOUGHT FLOW..........31

Positive Thought Flow............ 33

Real Estate Investing 35

Thinking About Money in a New Way 37

Ask a Better Question, Get a Better Answer 38

Changing Our Habits 40

CHAPTER 4

BALANCE—MIND, BODY AND SPIRIT 47

Deck Ten—Questioning My Beliefs 47

Big Mind, Small Mind 53

Four Noble Truths 55

Being Positive 56

Discovering Balance 57

CHAPTER 5

MONEY FOLLOWS THOUGHTS 61

You Are What You Think 62

Becoming an Entrepreneur 63

Coming back from the Abyss 66

CHAPTER 6

DO AND BE WHAT YOU LOVE 77

Finding Your Purpose Not Just Your Passion 80

The Right to be Rich 83

Stop Worrying—Start Living 84

Charting Your Course 86

CHAPTER 7

SUCCESS AND SIGNIFICANCE 107

Connie and Sheila Talk.............................. 108

The Same But Different............................. 110

Defining Success & Significance 112

Asking Better Questions 113

CHAPTER 8

OUR MINDS NEED REST **117**

A Season to Remember............................. 117

Therapy: It Does a Mind Good 120

They Are Not Forgotten............................ 121

The Thinking Rock Story 128

Seeds of Peace 130

CHAPTER 9

THE IMPETUS THAT MOVES US FORWARD..................**133**

Neighbor Jay... 133

The Aim of Living..................................... 135

Introduction to Universal Laws and Principles......... 137

Newton's Law of Universal Gravitation.................. 138

Newton's Laws of Motion 139

The Law of Cause and Effect 141

iPods, iTunes & iTalk............................... 143

CHAPTER 10

CONSCIOUS AWARENESS OF ALL THINGS 149

   Twinkling Presence and Midnight Skies 151

   Breathing Easy 153

   My Brother Mike's a Saint 154

   Thinking on Purpose 154

   The Big Iron 156

   THiNKING CONSCIOUSLY ROCKS! 157

   Keywords 159

CHAPTER 11

DREAMING AWAKE—VISION 163

   Designing Your Life (DYL) 167

   Dream Awake 168

   THiNK Vision by Creating a Vision Board 170

   What is a Vision Board? 170

   My Vision Board 172

CHAPTER 12

THINK GRATITUDE, PEACE, LOVE & THINK VISION ... 177

   p.e.ACE 179

EPILOGUE 184

DESCRIPTION OF YOUNG LADY/OLD LADY 185

ACKNOWLEDGEMENT 186

ABOUT THE AUTHOR..187

BIBLIOGRAPHY 188

RESOURCES..190

PRODUCTS...194

Foreword

We all dream of lives filled with happiness, meaning, and fulfillment. And yet, it seems that reality assures us that we will experience hardships as well. God has apparently designed us to grow from the unexpected struggles that inevitably show up. But, like the butterfly struggling to get out of the cocoon, our struggles are part of making us fully alive. And like the butterfly, those struggles are not intended to limit or cripple us, but to allow us to develop our resilience, fortitude, compassion, and personal excellence.

In this hopeful book, Connie Williams shares her own story of losing a loved one and how the pain of that experience trapped her in anger, fear, and depression. Her continued search for answers led her to discover that she was not trapped—she had a choice. She could move beyond those negative emotions to be more empathetic and joyous than ever before. Ultimately she discovered the brain research that shows how in brief, 90-second cycles each of us have the option to continue in or to release negative emotions.

Connie describes the process that helps us make the choices that renew our minds in positive ways. In the movie *Shadowlands*, C. S. Lewis describes the intense pain of losing his wife: "Why love if losing hurts so much? I have no answers any more. Only the life I have lived. Twice in that life I've been given the choice: as a boy and as a man. The boy chose safety, the man chooses suffering. The pain now is part of the happiness then. That's the deal."

It seems inevitable that loving deeply opens us up to the potential of deep pain as well. *Thinking Consciously Rocks!* guides us through the process of opening up after being wounded. Of trusting after trust has been violated or stretching in areas that culture and tradition have warned us against. Connie helps us understand what Maya Angelo meant in saying, "When you know better, you do better." This is a book to help us know, and do, better. Forgiveness, peace, hope, and compassion are characteristics that can be learned. Those healthy, spiritual traits may not seem natural in light of real-life circumstances but they can be learned in spite of those circumstances.

I challenge you to open your heart and discover how the unexplained and often unwelcomed events in our lives can move us toward the greatness intended for each of us. As we move away from our own hurts and fears, we release the best in ourselves and encourage the same in those around us.

I urge you to do something special for others and yourself— read *Thinking Consciously Rocks!* The investment of your time will come back multiplied with more personal light, joy, and victory and will illuminate the way for others whom you touch along the way.

Dan Miller, author and life coach (www.48Days.com)

Franklin, Tennessee

Author's Note

Thursday, April 21, 1994, was the day they told me my brother Carl was dead. He had been murdered the night before while walking along the shoulder of the interstate. His body was found lying about one mile from where his Nissan pickup truck had failed—his head lying in a pool of blood. The following morning the papers read, "A man was killed by a hit and run driver on I40 sometime Wednesday evening." By that afternoon the story had changed—from accidental death to cold-blooded murder.

Sometimes we might think life isn't fair. Things happen and we wonder how we'll ever survive. We question life asking, "How did this happen and why?"

Carl had the kind of smile that made you want to smile back. He loved to have fun and wanted everyone to enjoy life. His story has become a part of what makes me who I am. In one afternoon, the bitter feelings I held toward an unknown murderer turned into an unexplainable love.

Had I known my thoughts create my reality, I would have thought differently. I would not have suffered as long.

Our thoughts allow us to enjoy each day, or they prevent us from achieving the life we are entitled to. This is my story about murder, thinking differently, acquiring wealth, and finding peace. Throughout history, many successful people have experienced the creative energy and power contained in the mind. However, many never realize they possess such power. Utilizing the Law of Attraction, conscious thinking, and mindful action, we can live the life we've always dreamt of. Peace, joy, and abundance are ours for the asking. My grief hung around for over fifteen years after my brother was killed. It wasn't until I began changing the way I thought that I discovered the energy, the power, and the Source to live life fully.

For over 25 years I have been an entrepreneur. My partner and I have built a seven figure real estate portfolio. Only in the last couple of years have I understood how to harness the power within and design the life I want to live. Connecting with this inner power has changed my life. More importantly I have found peace—the peace that passes all understanding.

I can't explain how I can love the person who murdered my brother, maybe it's because I now know we are all one. What I do to another, I do to myself. Our thoughts keep us moving toward or away from greatness. The cool thing is—we decide what we think about. The better we think, the better we live. *THiNKING CONSCIOUSLY ROCKS!* and it can change your life.

Chapter 1

From Murder to Mindfulness
Seeing the good in everything

"It is not the mountain we conquer but ourselves."

~ Sir Edmund Hillary, 1919-2008

Thursday, April 21, 1994, was the day they told me my brother Carl was dead. He had been murdered the night before while walking along the shoulder of the interstate. His body was found lying about one mile from where his Nissan pickup had broken down—his head lying in a pool of blood.

The days following his murder were a confused, blurry nightmare. A permanent fog seemed to settle in my mind. I couldn't comprehend that this heinous crime had happened. My whole being was filled with pain, rage, and agony. I was numb; my body felt like it belonged to someone else. Time stood still for me, yet at the same time the world seemed to be spinning out of control. We buried my brother on Saturday, April 23.

As we waited for an arrest, days turned into weeks and weeks into months. The months then turned into years, and years turned into agony. Now, nearly two decades have passed since his untimely death, and Carl's murder remains unsolved. My parents had survived forty-two years of marriage; six children, ten grandchildren, financial stress, job loss, deaths, and every other thing a couple experiences in over four decades together—it didn't survive Carl's murder.

The senseless act of violence that took my brother's life at age thirty-two also took my father's life less than seven months later. He grieved himself to death. The year started on a Saturday, we buried Carl on a Saturday, and Dad died on a Saturday. I was 29 years old when Carl died. I turned 30 in August of 1994 and Dad died three months later in November—he was sixty-one years old. 1994, designated on the Gregorian calendar as a 'common year' was far from common for my family and me.

Growing Up

Carl had a great laugh and a gorgeous smile. He loved to have fun, was a practical jokester, and loved to tease people. He enjoyed anyone who enjoyed life. Perhaps that's why as a child I tried to follow my brother wherever he went.

There were six children in our family, three boys, and three girls. My parents, Charles and Mary, married in 1952—Mom was fourteen and Dad was nineteen. Two and a half years after they married they welcomed their first son, Charles Michael. Two years after Mike's birth came Cynthia Marlene, then, eleven months later Calvin Mark was born. Cheryl Melinda was born three years after Mark. Their fifth child, a little eight-pound bomb, that was my brother Carl Malcolm.

He was two-and-a-half when I was born. I am the baby. Sticking to the C for Charles and M for Mary, they named me Connie Michelle. Our family was close. Growing up in a three bedroom, one-bath house with eight people made us even closer.

The Bilskie family had four children and lived next door to our small house in southern Indiana. Together we played football and freeze tag, kickball, and other games in the lot that separated our houses. Since I was the baby, my siblings would give me to the neighbors to make the teams even, at least in numbers anyway. The Field's family lived down the street, on the corner. I got to be on the Williams team when we played with them, because they were like us—three girls and three boys.

About the time my siblings were finishing high school, starting careers or getting married, my parents bought a house in Nashville. That is when Carl began picking me to be on his team instead of trading me to the neighbors. He liked my competitive nature, and being a tomboy I played better than some of the boys. I liked being on my brother's flag football team, no longer having to play opposite him.

Our backyard had a built in pool, so if we weren't playing in the pool, we were playing in our neighbor's back yard with some of the neighborhood kids. When the sun went down it didn't stop us from playing.

When my parents bought the house in Nashville, the pool in the backyard looked like a swamp. There was nothing pretty about 15,000 gallons of dark, stinky water, with bullfrogs sitting atop old tires and croaking on algae. It took a lot of work, but we got the pool drained, cleaned, painted, and filled with sparkling clear water.

Sleeping soundly one night, Carl came into my room and

whispered, "Do you want to go for a swim?" Rubbing my eyes and asking him what time it was, he laughed and said, "It would be a midnight swim." He was already wearing his new purple swimming trunks, so I got up and got my suit on. He thought it would be fun to swim at night.

When we dove into the pool we didn't know three hours earlier Dad had poured gallon after gallon of straight bleach into the water. As our heads popped up out of the water we were both rubbing our eyes. The burning sensation was bad, but not bad enough to make us get out of the pool. Our midnight swim lasted less than an hour. Dad woke up and ran out to tell us, "Get out, I just poured a bunch of bleach in there." We laughed for years about the time we went swimming and our suits turned gray and our hair a little green and hay feeling.

With our parent's permission, Carl joined the Marines when he was seventeen. Everyone was growing up, moving away, starting their families, and living separate lives. I was the last child at home and was beginning to see how our family was changing. I was only fourteen.

Wednesday, April 20, 1994

Nashville's Assistant Medical Examiner determined Carl's death was a result of a hit-and-run. The following morning the papers read, "A man was killed by a hit and run driver on I40 sometime Wednesday evening."

My sister Cheryl heard the same announcement on the radio as she drove to work Thursday morning. She flashed back to the night before, ringing in her ears were my mother's words— *Carl isn't home yet.* Cheryl had called my parents Wednesday night to thank them and Carl for coming over to help with the new house.

Dad and Carl hung drywall in the house my sister Cheryl and

her husband were building. Mom and Dad left Cheryl's house about 7:30 p.m. Carl left twenty minutes later and was covered in drywall dust. When Mom got home that night she thought it was odd that Carl hadn't come straight home to shower. Carl had lived with my parent's since breaking up with his girlfriend a few months earlier. After Cheryl heard the story on the radio, she called our mother. She wanted to know what time Carl had gotten home the night before. What she really wanted to ask was, "Did Carl make it home?" When Mom said, "Carl never came home." Cheryl told Mom about the news report she had heard on the radio that morning. Minutes later my office phone rang. I heard my mother's teary voice say, "Honey, I think Carl may have been killed last night." At first the words didn't register. It took some time for my brain to process the words coming through the phone. I was so insulated I couldn't imagine the man found dead on the interstate could be Carl. By mid-morning, we still weren't sure about his whereabouts. Our hearts didn't want to believe there was any correlation between Carl's absence and the news story—but at some level we suspected what might come.

When Mom and I hung up, I called Cheryl. We decided to go to our parent's house because we shared the same sick feeling. We didn't want Mom to be alone if a Chaplin or detective knocked on the front door. On our way there we called our other siblings in town, Mike and Cindy, and asked them to meet us at our parent's house. Since our brother Mark lived in Minnesota we chose to call him after we knew more. Once we were with Mom, we tracked down our father at a doctor's appointment. We asked the receptionist at the doctor's office to please have him come home.

The Deceased Was Named Williams

Standing in my parent's breakfast room I made several phone

calls inquiring about the man killed on the interstate. The last call I made was to the coroner's office. I knew someone there and thought I might be able to find out if the victim was Carl. They didn't know I was related when I asked about the man. When they said the deceased was named Williams, I couldn't believe it. I gasped and heard them say, "Oh, Connie, are you related to him?" Instead of answering the question, I asked if there were any identifying marks on the victim's body" they said, "Yeah, there's an eagle tattoo on his bicep with the letters 'USMC' underneath it. My knees buckled. "Yes, that's my brother," I heard myself say.

Call waiting beeped, and I told them I had to take the other call. When I switched to the other line I heard the sorrowful voice of my friend. She worked for a local news channel and was returning my call. I told her I knew the man killed was Carl, but I was surprised when she said he'd been shot.

Dad was the last to arrive home and he was visibly shaken. Several of us were standing on the porch as he ran to the house asking, "Is it your mother?" He didn't know why he had been called home. Mike hugged him and said, "No Dad, its Carl. Someone shot him and he's dead." We had gone from believing Carl had been killed by a hit-and-run driver, to finding out that he had been murdered—shot in the head. How could this be happening?

The Detectives Arrive

Several hours passed before two detectives arrived to deliver the news. They confirmed that Carl was the man who had been killed on the interstate. We were told when the medical examiner x-rayed the body bag with my brother inside, (a routine procedure in this type of death); they were surprised by what they found. There was a bullet in his head and he had been shot at point blank range. It wasn't a hit and run, it was cold-blooded murder.

The Force That Drove Me to Write This Book

Around the fifteen-year anniversary of Carl's death, I began thinking about writing a book. I wanted to help people overcome the grief of having lost a loved one by homicide. What I didn't expect was what happened during the first few days of writing. I had been through years of grief counseling and spent hours with others who had lost loved ones to murder. As I began writing the book, I heard a voice—not audibly but powerfully in my spirit say *"You need to quit telling people what to do."* It was soft but sure, loud but kind and, it resonated deep-down in my being. I closed my laptop and sat for a long time—the words echoing in my mind.

I spent hours asking myself what this message meant. I often tell people what to do—not in a hateful way, but in a way that conveys that I think my way is better. Arrogant, right? I thought I was being helpful when I told people what to do. I think we all do.

The following day I took my mother to the doctor. As we walked into the office, Mom's shoulder purse was nearly dragging the ground. Seeing her shoulders slumped from carrying the heavy purse, I said "Hey Mom, you ought to…" then it hit me, I was about to tell someone what to do. I knew I couldn't continue so I stopped in mid-sentence.

Since that day, when I start to tell someone what to do, I feel like I've been hit with a stun gun. This is a not-so-gentle reminder to keep my opinions to myself. What's the lesson here? I now know to honor and respect each person I come into contact with, and allow them their own opinions. Who am I to make a judgment call for someone else?

I had evolved since Carl's death, but still I wondered if I was the right person to write this book. I continued writing and as I wrote, more and more questions arose. I began to see things differently. I was changing. I began to ask myself questions. *How did I get to this place in my life? Why do I believe what I believe?* I felt the only way to understand who I am, was to go back to the beginning.

The Growing Up Years

Mrs. Decker, who lived across the street, gave me my first job. I think of her as an older lady, but she was probably the age I am now. I was five years old, and everyone over twelve was old to me. I cut her grass each week with a reel mower. Reel mowers didn't have a motor, just several curved blades that turned as the mower was pushed. It probably wasn't safe for a five-year-old child to be using a mower, but it was the sixties. We didn't think about safety as much as we do today.

When I was finished cutting her postage stamp size yard she would give me a shiny quarter and a glass of lemonade. I liked getting this quarter each week. One of my older siblings would walk with me to the corner market and I'd buy some candy. This was the beginning of my need to make more money.

When I was nine my parents moved our family to Nashville. My father got a job in construction and was working for a builder in Brentwood. Money was still tight for our family and as the years passed and the older kids moved out, I began to see how tight things really were. My older siblings had been helping pay some of the bills. My parents never fought about money in front of me, but I knew there was financial stress in our home.

Wanting More

As a child I always wanted to have my own business and to be rich when I grew up. That was my dream. I never thought too much about where that dream came from, but as I got older I realized that the desire to be rich stemmed from knowing the financial stress which my parents endured. I didn't want to live from paycheck to paycheck. Since my parents couldn't afford to pay for certain things that I wanted, like new tennis shoes or a really cool tee-shirt, I would make money by selling candy at school. I would walk to the market and buy Now-or-Laters for five cents each and sell them for a quarter each. Each week I would buy 100 pieces of candy for five dollars and make a $15 profit. Did you catch the math? You might wonder where the other $5 went. It went to pay my brother Carl for walking with me to the store. It was 1975 and we had been in Nashville for a little over a year. My mother said it wasn't safe for me to walk alone. A young girl, my age, had been kidnapped and murdered in Greenhills, a neighborhood about ten miles from our house.

That little girl was Marcia Trimble. Today her mother Virginia Trimble Ritter is a good friend of mine. Virginia endured thirty-plus years of not knowing who killed her little girl. Through DNA and great police work, Marcia's killer was brought to justice on July 18, 2009. A jury convicted 62-year-old Jerome Barrett of two counts of second-degree murder. Barrett was sentenced to 44 years in prison. The Marcia Trimble case changed Nashville. Little girls couldn't walk alone—it wasn't safe. With my big brother, Carl, my protector, by my side we walked to the store so I could buy candy.

A couple of years later when I was in junior high and Carl was a sophomore, we figured out another way to make money. We would fish slimy golf balls out of the ponds at Two Rivers Golf Course. We'd scrub the balls, package them, and sell them as shag balls to the local golfers. Carl hung back and made me go do the selling. I used to think it was because he was lazy and wanted me to do all the work. But now I think it was because he knew golfers would be more likely to buy from a little girl than a teenage boy. I never got to give him credit for that, or tell him I finally figured out his strategy.

I tell you these childhood moneymaking stories so you will understand the magnitude of the next "message" I received while writing. As I typed the words, *I* remembered that as a child I wanted to have my own business. I want to be rich when I grew up. I heard the *voice* again. A voice, both quiet and thunderous penetrated my whole being. It said, "What is it with you and money? How much do you need? What are you going to do with all of it when you get it?" Boom, boom, boom—the questions rang through my mind. I was stunned. Why is this happening? I closed my laptop and repeated, "What is it with you and money? How much do you need? What are you going to do with all of it when you get it?" I spent the rest of the afternoon answering each question as honestly as I could.

As I sat answering the questions just posed to me, the realization hit me, I have everything I need. I have food, shelter, and clothing. I really don't NEED more money. Why do I need more money, when I have everything I need? A feeling of gratitude swept over me and I began to weep. I thanked God for all that I had. It was the first time in my life that I felt totally complete; my life was missing nothing. I had never been more present. As I sat and looked around, I became more and more thankful for my home, my clothes, and for my food. The three basic needs were met and always had been. Never once have I been homeless, not one time in my life did I not have clothes to wear. No matter how much my parents struggled financially, I never went to bed hungry. Why then did I have this obsession about making money?

After ruminating I concluded it was fear. Knowing I had spent my life with a goal to have my own business and to be rich made me feel shallow. Never before that day had I understood the depth of my gratitude for the things I had been blessed with. When I settled into the knowledge that I have everything I need, I became more grateful for my life and all that it encompassed. I sat in awe, in a peace that passes all understanding.

From Murder to Mindfulness

Hearing the two messages prompted me to dig deep inside myself to find the answers to those questions. I can't begin to explain how cathartic writing this book has been for me. As I peeled back the layers of conditioned beliefs, the more layers I found. I realized that I had come to a place I had never been before when I began to think of Carl's murder.

Having just basked in the light, love, and presence of the creator of the universe, Carl's murderer came to mind. Since the case is still an unsolved murder I have no face to attach to this crime. In the past when I would think of his murderer, all I could see was a shadowy silhouette.

This day, as I processed thoughts, the figure changed. I began to think of this person(s) as someone no different than me. I realized we are more alike than different. Who am I to judge this person for having killed my brother? What kind of life had he led that allowed him to willingly take the life of another? My heart began to ache for him. My heart swelled with love.

At first I thought it was forgiveness. But, I began to see that it was the process of self-forgiveness taking place. I realized I have willingly given away my power by allowing Carl's murderer to steal so much of my joy.

We are all human and we are driven by emotions. There is a process that we all go through when something bad happens.

The world-renowned psychiatrist, Elisabeth Kübler-Ross, M.D., introduced the five stages of grief in her book *On Death and Dying*. The stages, popularly known by the acronym DABDA include denial, anger, bargaining, depression, and acceptance. Kübler-Ross says no matter what causes a person to grieve, they will experience at least two of these five stages. She says that experiencing these stages can be like a roller-coaster ride—switching between stages. I rode that roller coaster of emotions for well over a decade and I am here to tell you, it is not a fun ride.

The amazing thing is—I chose to stay on the ride.

I rode through all five stages of grief at different times. I now believe we have a choice; in fact, I know we have a choice. That day, sitting at my writing desk, I knew I had to get off the horrific roller coaster ride. I had to delve deep into my inner-being and choose to let go of the anger, bitterness, and sadness—not just toward the killer, but toward me. I knew what I had to do. I shifted my thoughts from pain and anger to love and gratitude. The darkness left and I was filled with a light and love that I had never known. For the first time, the tears were not because my brother had died, I was crying for having had the opportunity to know him. Now when I think of Carl, instead of thinking of him surrounded by the darkness of murder, I think of him in the spirit of light.

I wondered what kind of life had the murderer lived? What kind of conditioning had he been subjected to? What in the world could be in a person's mind that would allow them to think it is okay to take the life of another? My conclusion was that the murderer could not have been in his right mind. He needed my love and not my hate. That was the last time I ever felt the need for the murderer to be arrested and sent to prison for what he had done. That part didn't matter to me anymore. Capturing the killer, a trial, and a prison sentence didn't matter.

I had been the one imprisoned, and now, I had received my freedom—from murder to mindfulness in one afternoon.

Chapter 2

The Same But Different
Honoring the polarity of our perceptions

"You must be the change you wish to see in the world."

~ Mohandas Karamchand Gandhi (1869-1948)

One man's trash is another man's treasure. You have probably heard that sometime in your life. Have you ever really thought much about the message in that old saying? How can something have so little value to one person that they are willing to throw it away—yet to another person that same garbage is a treasure?

So which is it, something of value or something without value? How can we answer that question? Is it possible for both to be right? Can something be considered of value in one person's mind, while worthless in another man's mind? Yes, it can.

We don't all see and process things the same way. Why should we? We have not all had the same life experiences. Who we are today is a direct result of our past experiences. We are different because of our family beliefs, environment, culture, the schools we attended, the neighbors we played with, or the churches, synagogues, or mosques we attended or choose not to attend.

Some experiences can misshape us, but our thoughts can shape or misshape us as well. You don't have to be a nueroanatomist to know the human brain is an amazing and intricate organ. The brain is the center of our nervous system, which coordinates all the actions we take. We all perceive and evaluate circumstances differently.

Here is a simple example of how we can look at the same thing and see it differently. I found this picture in a book I was reading years ago. I was surprised when the book talked about an old lady in the picture. When I look at this picture, I see a young lady. I could not see the old lady, so I showed the picture to my partner Sheila and asked her what she saw. She looked at me kind of funny and said, "An old lady—why? What's the catch?"

I laughed and said, "Really, you see an old lady?"

"Yes, what am I supposed to see? What do you see?"

When I told her I saw a young lady, Sheila got the same look on her face that I am sure I had when she said she saw an old lady. Funny thing is, Sheila and I are a lot alike, but we understand we don't always see things the same way. We began using this picture in classes that we teach on real estate investing, to show people how two people can look at the same picture, event, or opportunity, differently.

"My Wife and My Mother-in-Law," by cartoonist W.E. Hill 1915

So what is it? What do you see, an old lady, or a young lady? If you only see one or the other, blink, move the book to a different angle, think differently. Look with different eyes. After you've seen both the old lady and the young, you'll probably switch back and forth seeing both. Most people always have a dominant view pop up first, but eventually they can see both images.

After seeing so many people in our classes react to this drawing, I was happy to see how people laughed when they saw both views. "That's weird," they'd say. When we understand we don't always see things as others do, it is much easier to laugh at our own conditioning. Using this picture taught Sheila and me that we can each see the same thing, but differently.

Honoring the polarity of our perceptions became our new goal. We could settle a lot of disagreements with saying, "Hey, it's just an old lady, young lady thing." Knowing we were just seeing things differently and there really was no right or wrong.

I never read a book in high school. Prior to 2003, when I was thirty-nine years old, I can only remember having read one entire book. When I was in kindergarten at Vigo Elementary School I must have checked out *Are You My Mother?* fifty times. I loved that book. Why? I don't know. My reading habits and my life began to change in 2003.

New Influences

In 2003 Sheila bought Robert Kiyosaki's book, *Rich Dad, Poor Dad*. I was drawn to that book and I read it in three days. I shared the content of the book with Sheila and within days we were doing what Kiyosaki suggested, we began to educate ourselves. We saw a full-page ad in *The Tennessean* for a wealth-building seminar that was coming to town. Since we were interested in learning how to make money, we called the number on the ad and made our reservations. At that seminar we met a couple named Greg and Ginny Pitts. They were real estate investors, and lived about eight miles from us. We were fascinated by this couple and wanted to learn more about them and their business.

At that time Sheila and I had our own advertising specialty business. We were losing our passion for this type of business and we were actively looking for something different. We knew selling embroidered caps and golf shirts when we were sixty was not going to cut it. We wanted and needed a better plan for our retirement. We were thankful for the advertising specialty business Sam and Martha Sanders (our business mentors and friends), helped us start in 1994. We longed for something that would give us more than a J-O-B.

Greg and Ginny became our mentors in January 2004. In April 2004 we purchased our first rental property. Since then we have bought, rehabbed, sold, or kept as rental property, over one hundred properties. In about six years we went from making a five figure income and having a five figure net worth, to making a six figure income and having a seven figure net worth.

It still blows my mind that investing in real estate can make you a millionaire in such a short period of time. Not everyone thinks real estate is a safe investment these days. To that I say—it is just an old-lady-young-lady thing. I truly believe if we had not read Kiyosaki's *Rich Dad, Poor Dad* we would not be where we are today.

Kiyosaki's book gave me an insatiable thirst for knowledge. I read all of his *Rich Dad* series. I then began devouring books on how to make money, time management, and goal setting. I have read books by Brian Tracy, Tony Robbins, Zig Ziglar, and many others. Most of what I read and enjoyed was about business and making money.

Learning Acceptance

Through real estate investing Sheila and I met a couple named Steve and DeeDee Brickner. They are a fun, sweet couple. (Ironically they live across the street from where Marcia Trimble disappeared in 1975. Her body was found 33 days later not far from where she lived.) Steve bought the house sometime in the 80's, before he and DeeDee were married. As our friendship grew, Steve and DeeDee invited Sheila and me to go on a mission trip to Honduras with them and their Sunday school class. The Methodist church they attended had planned a medical mission trip in conjunction with the non-profit organization, Heifer International. We were told there were about twelve people going this particular year.

We wanted to go, but were a little uncomfortable going with a group from a church that didn't know us. I told DeeDee before we would consider going we had to know if the group would be okay with Sheila and me. Steve and DeeDee assured me we were welcome. Sheila and I became a couple in 1986 and are as committed today as we were 25 years ago. We wanted the group to know about us because a lot of people in church don't take too kindly to gay people. DeeDee spoke to the group and everyone was cool with us going along to Honduras.

A few months passed. The week before we were to leave for the mission trip we found ourselves in Sunday school with Steve and DeeDee. After Sunday school we all packed the suitcases for our stay in Honduras. The bags were filled with medicine, clothes, games for children, and whatever else we could take.

It was the first time Sheila and I had met the rest of the group. We felt welcomed and excited to be a part of this endeavor. The trip was amazing. We spent 10 days crossing Honduras, from San Pedro Sula to Tegucigalpa, then Quebrada Honda to Copan. Each day we fell more in love with the Honduran people.

Being a gay couple in the south is not a popular thing with everyone. Sheila and I are very kind and loving people and we always hope people see that in us and the Nashville group did. They treated us with such grace and respect—we genuinely felt their love.

I believe God puts us exactly where we need to be at all times. This trip was great for us and I have to believe we were there for several reasons. There were two people in our group that had a gay child. They were struggling with this new-found knowledge and asked us a lot of questions. They told us they were glad Steve and DeeDee had invited us. They said being around Sheila and me helped them to better understand their child.

When Sheila and I met in 1986, neither of us had dated another woman. Some people think being gay is wrong. Heck, I did for the first three years I was with Sheila. I was raised in a Christian home and being gay would send you straight to hell. That is the way I grew up. Imagine my turmoil when I found myself involved with a woman.

The Same but Different

It took me a while to overcome the conditioned belief that I would be sent to hell for being in love with a woman. The longer I was with Sheila the less this made sense to me. How could God, the creator of love, punish me for loving? It took a while for me to unlearn all the teachings of my youth. I heard this joke once, *I'm not gay, but my girlfriend is*. That is the way I felt for the first few years of our relationship. I had to wrap my brain around it and open my heart to know that I am who I am, and I am gay.

We are all taught some pretty unbelievable things. There is so much fear and judgment passed down through generations. I wonder why we never have taken time to stop and ask ourselves, "What do I believe"?

We believe what we believe sometimes through conditioning, sometimes through blind acceptance. Sometimes we don't take the time to think it through. That's how it was for me. It wasn't until I started asking myself the question "Why do I believe what I believe?" that I was able to break free from that learned behavior.

In the fifteenth century people thought women with red hair were witches. Red hair and green eyes meant they could be a werewolf. Do you see how crazy some beliefs can be? When we continue to pass down absurd teachings and share in the discrimination of others, we can perpetuate myths and superstition.

Thankfully red heads are not thought of as witches or werewolves today. Inter-racial relationships are becoming more widely accepted. I think the same thing is true about people being gay. Many parts of the world are beginning to understand we are the same but different.

The title of this chapter, *The Same but Different* is a Sheilaism that I love. The first time I ever heard her say that, she said it like I should know exactly what she meant. The same but different, it twisted my brain a bit, but then I realized what she meant. If you think about it; we are all the same but different— more alike than different. For some reason though instead of focusing on the vast amount of things we have in common as human beings, we hone in on the differences.

Here is my challenge to you. When something makes you feel uncomfortable inside, whether its frustration, anger, or sadness, stop and ask yourself, "Where is this feeling coming from? Is it from your heart or your head?" Thinking with our head gets us in trouble a whole lot more than thinking from our hearts ever will.

Writing this book has been one of the most transforming things in my life because it inspired me to ask questions about what I believe. When I first considered writing a book I was uneasy. I was not a good student in high school and I had done most of my reading only within the last decade.

Today, I know the books I read and what I learn from them must be used for my own personal growth and nothing more. I don't feel like I have to tell anyone what to do because I read it in a book.

I realize now what resonates with me may not resonate with someone else. Now I like to share my gleanings without preaching. There are two books that I want to share with you because the information in them changed my life.

The first book that made my mind cramp was *My Stroke of Insight* by Dr. Jill Bolte Taylor. I first saw her on the Oprah.com Spirit Channel. In May 2008, Oprah released the interviews with Dr. Jill Bolte Taylor in a four-part series on the Oprah's Soul Series on XM Radio and Orpah.com. I didn't see it until the spring of 2009.

In the interviews the doctor explained what happened to her and how the experience helped her realize that we decide how we respond to hardships and obstacles in our lives. This made me think about my emotions in a whole new way. The following is taken from the website www.goodreads.com and it is a review of *My Stroke of Insight: A Brain Scientist's Personal Journey.*

On December 10, 1996, Jill Bolte Taylor, a thirty-seven-year-old Harvard-trained brain scientist experienced a massive stroke in the left hemisphere of her brain. For Taylor, her stroke was a blessing and a revelation. It taught her that by "stepping to the right" of our left brains, we can uncover feelings of well-being that are often sidelined by "brain chatter." Reaching wide audiences through her talk at the

Technology, Entertainment, Design (TED) conference and her appearance on Oprah's online Soul Series, Taylor provides a valuable recovery guide for those touched by brain injury and an inspiring testimony that inner peace is accessible to anyone.

www.goodreads.com/book/show/142292.My_Stroke_of _Insight

I am so thankful to Dr. Jill Bolte Taylor, for having the courage to fight her way back to health through a grueling eight-year process; but also for having the courage to share her story through her book. While I found the terminology and procedures complex, I got a most valuable lesson from it. She shares that our brain processes emotions in a physiological way that runs a pattern through our body in a 90 second loop.

We are human beings. We are going to get angry, depressed, or jealous. Think about your brain and body running the full gamut of emotions in 90 seconds. If, after 90 seconds, you are still suffering from that negative emotion it is because you are choosing to replay it again and again in your mind. Basically, you are asking your brain to run it through another loop. Around and around, throughout our bodies we choose to run anger, hate, sadness, isolation, bitterness, and a whole host of other negative emotions. This spoke to me like nothing I had ever read before.

Are we in control of our feelings and emotions after the initial physiological response? I thought of how my body reacts when I am in a near car accident. Your body tingles all over, every nerve ending firing. You might feel weak or nauseated, but the feeling doesn't last. The physiological response started when you realized you were almost in an accident and the brain made the 90-second loop. The cause and effect is over quickly and, you let go of the experience. You stop playing it over and over in your mind. The feelings don't hang around because you choose not to hold on to the emotion.

When we experience an emotion like anger or sadness, the feelings don't come and go as quickly. When we experience these negative emotions, if we don't let them go we risk repeating the experience by running the 90-second loop over and over again. We hit replay, years can pass and we are still living back in the day when the first 90-second response happened, not really knowing what we were doing.

We do have a choice. I began to observe my negative reactions. I practiced letting the emotion run its loop, and if after 90 seconds I was still experiencing the same emotion, knowing I had a choice helped bring me out of the negative loop. I found there is power in knowing we have a choice over our emotions, maybe not in the first 90 seconds, but afterwards. Knowing this and practicing this helped me release my negative feelings. I don't like the way they feel in my body and I would rather move on as quickly as possible through the process of negativity.

After reading *My Stroke of Insight* I became fascinated with neuroscience, the complexity of the human brain, and the power of mind over matter. The brain and how it functions is above my level of expertise, but I am smart enough to know that if I can control the need to be "right," I can choose to think differently and let go of emotions that steal my joy.

This I owe to Dr. Jill Bolte Taylor for her triumphant story. *My Stroke of Insight* showed me that we are all the same but different. Normal functioning brains involuntarily process emotions the same way for the first ninety seconds. Then the process turns from involuntary to voluntarily, and that is where we are different. Some of us hold on to things longer than others. This is why some people allow problems to roll off of them like water, while others dive into the problem and get soaked in a sea of negativity. We have to choose which emotions or thoughts we want to replay.

The other book I want to share with you is *Loving What Is: Four Questions That Can Change Your Life* by Byron Katie. R

From the website www.goodreads.com:

> *Out of nowhere, like a fresh breeze in a marketplace crowded with advice on what to believe, comes Byron Katie and what she calls "The Work." The Work is four questions that, when applied to a specific problem; enable you to see what is troubling you in an entirely different light. As Katie says, "It's not the problem that causes our suffering; it's our thinking about the problem."*
>
> *Many people have discovered The Work's power to solve problems; in addition, they say that through The Work they experience a sense of lasting peace and find the clarity and energy to act, even in situations that had previously seemed impossible.*
>
> *www.goodreads.com/book/show/9762.Loving_What_Is*

If I could give everyone in America a book, this would be the one. I love using "The Work." When facing a challenge in your life, asking and answering Katie's four questions will help you to see the problem more clearly. Here are the four questions. If you ask and answer them honestly the answers can change the way you think about any problem. For example the statement: Carl's murder was senseless and *should* never have happened.

Doing "The Work":

1. Is it true?

2. Can you absolutely know that it's true?

3. How do you react, what happens, when you believe that thought?

4. Who would you be without the thought?

Is it true? Carl's murder should never have happened. Can I really say what should and should not happen? I am not God and I cannot control what happens in other people's lives. But I want to say *yes*, that it's true, it should never have happened.

Can I absolutely know that it's true? I cannot absolutely know that it's true; but I want to say that I absolutely know that Carl's murder should never have happened. But who am I to make that call? I don't control the universe or the lives of others. I think the majority of people believe murder is a violent act and it should never happen to anyone, but it does. People shouldn't get cancer, but they do. Children shouldn't be abused, but they are. Marriages shouldn't end in divorce, but many do. I cannot know for sure what should or shouldn't happen. I believe that murder should never happen. But it does.

How do you react—what happens, when you believe that thought? When I believe the thought that Carl's murder should never have happened, it makes me sad. I feel angry and my heart races. I miss my brother; I want him to be here among us again. I think his life shouldn't have been cut short at the young age of 32. It doesn't make sense that someone would shoot him in the head. The thought, *Carl's murder should never have happened*, stirs up all kinds of emotions within me. Emotions that make me feel, sad, angry, and depressed.

Who would you be without the thought? When I lose the thought, *Carl's murder should never have happened*—does that mean he wasn't murdered? Does it mean I can change the reality that my brother was murdered? (Okay I got it, I think.) If I quit thinking that Carl should never have been murdered and accept the fact that he was, I can begin to move on? I can get unstuck. Get out of the rut. It is what it is and I cannot change it. I cannot change the past. I can only change the way I think about the past and how I allow those thoughts to dictate my moods.

I have actually been able to cut the process down by asking myself, why am I arguing with reality? Arguing with reality is insane. For instance, it's raining and I wish it weren't—many people get upset if the rain interferes with their plans. Really? Are we going to get mad because it's raining? Can we do anything about that? No! We must understand it is what it is. This moment is reality and we will always suffer if we want things to be different than they are right now.

Right now I know that Carl was murdered. For all those years I allowed my thoughts to be *it should have never happened, he shouldn't have been killed.* I now know I was torturing myself. I kept all the pain, depression and all of the negative emotions replaying in my brain.

I continued to hit the replay button. Every time I did that it was like saying I want things to be different than the way they are. I don't want this murder to be true. I want a different reality. I was trying to change the past. Until we change the way we think and quit trying to change reality, we will suffer. When we let go of trying to change "what is," we find ourselves moving into the fifth stage of Kübler-Ross's five stages of grief—acceptance.

When we accept reality, we begin to understand the power of now. Acceptance is much more peaceful, it is the place we all want to be and it can only be found in the Now. We struggle in finding our way there. It takes time for our minds to wrap around the reality and the finality of death. When we do, we find peace. Acknowledging reality diminishes suffering. No longer thinking what should or shouldn't have happened—we can find comfort in the present.

The other diamond I got from Byron Katie's book, *Loving What Is*, is her insightful teaching W*hose business are you in?* Katie says there are three businesses; yours, God's and mine. If I get upset about something, I need to ask myself the question, *Whose business am I in?* The rain for instance, isn't my business, but God's. The total number of days my brother was allowed to live—not my business. How much my mother's purse weighs is not my business, but hers. When we ask, "Why doesn't she do this or that?" or "Why won't he do what I want?" whose business are we really in? I think this is why the message I received of q*uit telling people what to do*, was so important to me.

It isn't other people and what they do that causes us to feel negative emotions, it is our negative emotional response to what they do. When we experience negative emotions because we want something to be different than it is, we are in someone else's business, and causing our own pain and frustration.

When I mind my own business and I am not telling people what to do and when I quit wanting things to be different than they are; I am much more peaceful. When we choose to rerun the loop of bad emotions, and refuse to think consciously and be present in the Now, we are giving away our power. This allows the words and actions of people or circumstances to rob us of our joy and peace.

Please don't misunderstand me. I am not saying that I think our reality can change. This moment is reality—the next moment is what we make it. We cannot change the past, but we can change our present and future. We are the same but different. All of us can change our future; the difference is that only some of us will. If we don't like the life we are living, our present and future can change by the actions we take. The Swiss psychiatrist and influential thinker Carl Jung once said, "What you resist persists." We have the power to change everything about our lives by changing the way we think.

I began this chapter with the quote by Gandhi that says, "Be the change you want to see in the world." I repeat this quotation often, but I change the words slightly. I must be the change I want to see in my life. If my life is ever going to change, it will be me that changes it.

Gandhi also said, "Truth resides in every human heart, and one has to search for it there and to be guided by truth as one sees it. But no one has a right to coerce others to act according to his own view of truth."

Chapter 3

Changing Our Thought Flow

Things are not always as they appear

> *"Begin to see yourself as a soul with a body versus a body with a soul."*
>
> ~Dr. Wayne Dyer

There is something special about a group of people you can spend ten days in the mountains of Honduras with and when you get home; you want to spend more time with them. We had bonded. Upon our return home from Honduras in July 2008, we were officially invited to attend the Sunday school class. They joked and said, "We meet in the basement of the church and we aren't like a real Sunday school class. We're more like a book club. In fact, the next book we're studying is Eckhart Tolle's, *The Power of Now: A Guide to Spiritual Enlightenment*."

I had never heard of Eckhart Tolle, but we decided to go to the class. It wasn't long before I learned Oprah had just begun a world-wide-web class with Tolle covering his new book, *A New Earth: The Power of Now.* Here is a book review from www.goodreads.com.

> *Ekhart Tolle's message is simple: living in the now is the truest path to happiness and enlightenment...Tolle is a world-class teacher, able to explain complicated concepts in concrete language. Tolle packs a lot of information and inspirational ideas into The Power of Now. (Topics include the source of Chi, enlightened relationships, creative use of the mind, permanence and the cycle of life.)*
>
> Gail Hudson
>
> *www.goodreads.com/book/show/6708.The_Power_of_ Now*

The more I read, the more I learn about personal development. The teachings, messages and lessons motivational speakers, and inspirational leaders share are from their personal experiences. For something to really take hold I think we have to make it personal. This is where personal development begins.

Many times in the past I would try to take expert's words and make them work for me. For some reason, they never totally worked. The reason is I was trying to do what worked for them. We each have a story and when we can use positive messages to help us find our truth, we are on the path to evolving personally. When we try to do what people tell us to do, however, we just wind up frustrated and feeling like nothing works.

THiNKing CONSCIOUSLY ROCKS! will resonate with some—but not all. I will be thrilled if one third of the people who read this book love it, one third hate it and the other third could care less. That would be a great success for me. We are all different—one message doesn't fit all. Until we take the time to think for ourselves and figure out what works for us, we will continue to look to others for a solution to our problem.

Positive Thought Flow

For years I couldn't get passed the anger, and sadness of losing my brother. I tried counseling and even though that helped, the pain was still there. It wasn't until I began changing the flow of thoughts that the pain from Carl's death began to subside. We all search for inner peace. I began to understand I was the block—I was the reason I didn't have inner peace.

For many years I had unconsciously been running that repetitive loop, I call it my JBT (Jill Bolte Taylor) loop. We cannot change something until we go inside and find the root of the problem. I guarantee whatever the obstacles in your life, if you go inside you will find the roadblock. Do I wish Carl had never been murdered? Yes! I wish he could have had a longer life, but it is beyond my control. When I long for something that cannot be, I bring on my own suffering. Wanting something to be different causes pain, we are arguing with reality and we are in someone else's business. To have peace of mind, we must shift our thoughts from negative to positive, and into a place of reality. This very moment is where changes can occur.

When I read *The Power of Now* with the Sunday school group, it was mind blowing. The essence of Tolle's book is being in the present—and being present takes practice. Living consciously and being present is something most of us have not been taught. *The Power of Now* by Tolle is a controversial book. But as long as the public disputes and debates who is right and who is wrong, any book about God, spirituality, the universe, and all of creation will be controversial. Tolle's words began to seep into my mind. His message was far from anything I had ever been taught. It took a while for my mind to catch up.

> *For my 30th birthday Sheila took me skydiving. I experienced an odd sensation when jumping out of the plane—my physical body was falling at the rate of 160mph toward earth, while my mind was still hanging back in the plane. It took a few seconds for my mind to catch up with my body before the disorienting feeling dissipated. I felt this same feeling when first reading Tolle's book.*

I began to notice any time I was not feeling happy; my thoughts were about other people's business or someplace other than in the moment. If I felt depressed it was over something in the past, something that had already happened. I was stuck in yesterday. When I felt worried, it stemmed from thoughts about the future, about what may, or may not happen. I was stuck in tomorrow.

I realized the life that goes on in my mind was living in the past and the future, but seldom were my thoughts in the present. I began trying to live in the NOW. It was difficult at first. It took practice.

Why is it so difficult to stay in the present? Some research suggests that eighty percent of our thinking is negative. I researched how many thoughts per day a person has and was surprised by my findings. Although opinions varied widely, some experts say people have as few as 12,000 thoughts per day, while others believe people have 60,000 thoughts per day or more. Do deep thinkers have fewer thoughts because they are so focused?

Do people who have 60,000 thoughts per day have five times as many thoughts because their minds run wild? Does the higher number of thoughts per day indicate a higher IQ? Perhaps the most important thing is not how many thoughts you have per day, but the quality of those thoughts.

I began to work hard at shifting my thoughts from negative to positive. The more positive thoughts I had, the better day I experienced. Positive thinking is the only way to produce positive results. If I want to be better, I have to become a better thinker. When I control my thinking I find more things in life to be grateful for. When I think gratitude it is far easier for me to be in the present.

Real Estate Investing

In January 2004, Sheila and I began our real estate investment training under the expert guidance of Greg and Ginny Pitts. One day while at their office, Greg mentioned a cruise they were taking and asked us to join them. Each year in February the National Real Estate Investors Association hosts an annual conference onboard a luxury cruise-liner. They shared the itinerary for the week and encouraged us to participate. Greg and Ginny took the cruise each year and thought it was well worth the money. Having just paid Greg and Ginny $1800 to teach us the business, Sheila, and I were reluctant to spend more money on real estate investing until we had actually made some money investing in real estate. Greg and Ginny understood and said, "Maybe next year."

As the months passed and we learned how to buy property, we found ourselves at the end of the year holding three rental properties. One day Greg asked if we were planning on going on the cruise in February. Even though we had picked up some rental property, increased our net worth, and bought and rehabbed our first project doing exactly what they taught us, we felt we couldn't afford to go. When we told Greg we didn't think we could afford it, he removed his aviator glasses (he's a pilot) and looked us in the eyes and said, "Girls you can't afford not to go. Ask yourself, how can we afford to go?" Now that is positive thought flow.

We were apprehensive about spending the $2500-$3000 it would cost us to go, but we restricted our thoughts to *how can we make this happen*? We believed that we should take the step of faith and go to the conference, even if it meant charging it to a credit card. We set sail that next February out of New Orleans and from there to Jamaica, Grand Cayman Islands, and Cozumel—it was amazing. Each day at sea we sat in classes while real estate experts shared their stories of success and offered programs for sale.

While docked in ports, I couldn't believe the beauty of the land all around us. We spent the day touring exotic places. This was the life. This was living the dream. Five hundred real estate investors were onboard; twenty of them were from Nashville. At home a normal week was busy and filled with meetings, the hustle and bustle of work and getting things done which left little time to get to know other investors.

While onboard the Carnival Miracle, (that really is the name of the ship) we were able to spend time with other investors from our own local market. Friendships were blossoming and we were excited to get home and use all the great information we were learning. We wouldn't have been able to go on this trip had we not changed our negative thought flow from we can't afford to go—to, how *can* we afford to go.

That was a big lesson for me. The whole trip was a miracle. The inspiration and knowledge we gained allowed us to more than double the number of properties we purchased that year. Over the years we have become friends with many people on that cruise. In fact some of our closest friends are people we got to spend seven days with, onboard a Carnival Fun Ship.

Thinking About Money in a New Way

After the 2005 cruise, Sheila and I changed the way we thought about money. Every time we thought, *we can't afford it*, we changed our thought flow to, *how can we afford to do this, how can we make this happen?* This is a powerful way of thinking. Too often, we think about what we can't do, instead of thinking about what we can do. Why do we think so negatively?

Several years ago I couldn't answer that question, but today I can and I am happy to share it with you. We think negatively because we don't know what we want. We under estimate our potential and we don't believe in others or ourselves. As we grow into adults we lose our dreams, life takes over, and before we know it we are middle aged and don't even know what we like anymore. We have lost our passion and are living day-to-day, but not day-to-day in a conscious sort of way—rather living a life driven by habit and routine. Like the 1993 movie Groundhog Day, where Bill Murray plays a weatherman and until he re-examines his life's priorities, he finds himself living the same day over and over again.

In 2006, that movie was added to the United Sates National Film Registry as being deemed "culturally, historically, or aesthetically significant." Why? I think because it resonated with most people who saw it. The significance is too many people feel their lives are in the control of others. We must reexamine our life and rediscover our dreams and passions. We must take action and bring the life we want to live into existence.

Ask a Better Question, Get a Better Answer

We have to ask ourselves new questions. We must get back to the days when we actually had passions, dreams, and goals. Applying Positive Thought Flow is asking the hard questions and then honestly answering each one and analyzing those answers. If the answers are negative, full of I can't, or it will never happen, or why did this have to happen, we won't move forward. Understand, as long as you are swimming in a sea of negativity, positive outcomes are impossible. I learned to shift my thoughts. Instead of asking why did this happen, I ask, "What can I learn from this?" Instead of saying I can't afford it, I ask, "How can I afford this or how can I make this happen?"

As I began to change the way I think, amazing things began happening. Opportunities were everywhere. People and things were coming into my life out of nowhere. I don't want to mislead you—and present this in a way that I had nothing to do with it, I did. I read a lot and I learned a lot. I did a lot of thinking and then I took action on those thoughts. Although the process didn't happen overnight—my life began to change.

Positive Thought Flow is a process. It takes time to break out of old habits, patterns and beliefs. What many of us have come to know as normal, often times is not normal. It is not normal for 80 percent of our thinking to be negative. Life is not supposed to feel like each day is the same as before.

I was watching an episode of Dr. Phil one day and was surprised by how moved I was with his opening introduction. This intro was part of the opening credits. You couldn't see him; you could only hear him say, "I want you to get excited about your life." I got chills. That is what so many of us are missing. Our lives have become so routine, so commonplace, that we have lost our zest for life. We need to find a way to get the excitement back. Our zeal for each day needs to be rejuvenated.

It is our birthright to be happy and live a life filled with passion, abundance, and peace—but we screw it up. We mess up our lives with our negative thinking. I want to encourage you to pay attention to your thoughts. When you notice having thoughts that are not kind, if you are tearing yourself down with negative self talk—stop. If you are talking badly about others, gossiping, wondering why *they* don't do this or that? Stop the negative thinking and give yourself time to go to your inner self and find a way to turn that negative thought into a positive one.

If it is your finances you are worried about, think of all you do have. Being grateful for the things we have will attract more good things. Worrying about bills or not having enough money attracts more things to worry about. If you are ill, instead of talking about being sick, be thankful for the healthy parts of your body. Not everybody part is dysfunctional; give thanks for the parts that are working properly. Being grateful for your smile, your eyes, your hair, your muscle tone, this helps shift negative thoughts to positive thoughts.

The glass is either half-empty, or half-full—you get to decide. For a long time I struggled with my body image. It seems I've always wanted to lose about 20 pounds. I fluctuate between sizes 8–14. My weight may be anywhere from 140-170, huge difference right? For years this bothered me, to a point where I was unhappy with my body. Today, I know my weight is what it is. Yes, I try to stay around a size 10 but when I am not, it doesn't make me unhappy. My life is not a wreck because I can't fit into my favorite jeans. It is what it is. When we begin to change the way we think and what we focus our thoughts on, our lives begin to change as well. *What we think about comes about.* The difficult part is noticing our thoughts and doing something about them.

Changing Our Habits

I started smoking when I was 17 years old. Twelve years ago when I was 35, I decided it was time to quit. After trying on my own and failing, I answered a hypnotist's ad in the paper that said, "Smoking Cessation Guaranteed." I quit after the first visit. Years passed and little by little the desire started to creep back in. I struggled with the urge to smoke for about five years. I would bum cigarettes, thinking somehow if I wasn't actually buying a pack I hadn't really started back. I found myself driving to a market, not to buy a pack of cigarettes, but to sit and wait until someone came out with a pack. When they did, I bummed one.

As they reached the pack toward me, I offered to pay for one cigarette. They would laugh and say, "No way man, I know what trying to quit is like, just take one." I eventually caved and began buying cigarettes again. I was once again a full-time smoker and I hated it. I didn't like the taste it left in my mouth, the smell on my hands, or in my hair and clothes. I knew I really didn't want to smoke but the addiction had such a hold on me that I continued to struggle with it for a year or more.

Finally, I decided to go visit a hypnotist and hope for the success I had achieved the first time. I didn't remember the first guy I went to so I found another hypnotist. I found M.C. Radford in Nashville. I went to him several times, not because it didn't work, but because we sat and talked the whole time, he told me "all illness starts in the mind." This old guy said things that I was only just learning about. We talked about the Law of

Attraction and Rhonda Byrne's best-selling book, *The Secret*. M.C. Radford had been helping people for over fifty years. He said, "People's problems are nothing more than thinking problems."

He gave me several books to read about metaphysics. He told me we manifest our life. He told me our lives are the way they are because of the way we think. He suggested I get a book called *The Master Key System* by Charles Haanel. I visited with M.C. Radford four times. In the next to the last session, after thirty minutes under hypnosis I quit smoking. I went back to see Mr. Radford one more time, just to talk. I paid him $85 an hour as a hypnotist and wound up feeling like I had been to a psychologist. The first two visits we talked about the power of the mind, the third visit, he cured me, and the last visit was just to talk again. Until writing this section, I haven't thought much about him in years. Maybe I'll look him up and share *THiNKING CONSCIOUSLY ROCKS!* with him.

I share this story with you, not to share my addictions but to say I know the mind is so very powerful. I know now we don't have to go to a hypnotist to go to a mental place where changes can happen. We can "hypnotize" ourselves. Hypnosis is not a form of unconsciousness or sleepy state. It is being fully awake and focusing our attention on what we want instead of what we don't want. It is shifting our thoughts from, "I don't want to smoke," or "I hate being a smoker" to "I love being healthy. I know I can do it." We attract reality by what we think so we must shift our thoughts to what we want, versus thinking what we don't want.

M.C. Radford said *The Master Key System* was an old book and he doubted it was still in print. After finding it online and printing a PDF version and making my very own three-ring binder of the book, imagine my surprise when Sheila bought us each a copy at Barnes & Noble. *The Master Key System* was originally published in 1912 as a 24-week correspondence course and was later released as a book in 1916. Rumor has it that in 1933 the Roman Catholic Church banned the book and it went out of print. Some say that Bill Gates discovered the book while in college and was so inspired that he dropped out of Harvard. He went on to found Microsoft.

The things Charles Haanel wrote 100 years ago are still relevant today. The book taught me that we have to find our own personal strategy for a successful life which comes from inside each one of us. I believe it all starts with the way we think. The better I think, the better my day is. The more conscious I am of my thoughts, the more kind, and loving I am. My thoughts (positive or negative) direct my next action. *THINKING CONSCIOUSLY ROCKS!* keeps me conscious of my thoughts and that works for me. I believe the impetus behind the *THINKING CONSCIOUSLY ROCKS!* message can transform lives.

What we are today is due to yesterday's thoughts while our present thoughts shape our tomorrows. Our life is created in our minds. Since *The Master Key System* was originally released as a twenty-four-week course, each student had one week to study and practice the lesson. When the book was originally released, this was the introduction:

> *The reader, who now receives the whole twenty-four parts at one time, is warned not to attempt to read the book like a novel, but to treat it as a course of study and conscientiously imbibe the meaning of each part—reading and re-reading one part only per week before proceeding to the next. Otherwise the later parts will tend to be misunderstood and the reader's time and money will be wasted.*

Being the great student that I wasn't, I didn't follow the instructions to go one week at a time. In the first week the lesson was:

> *Select a room where you can be alone and undisturbed; sit erect, comfortably, but do not lounge; let your thoughts roam where they will but be perfectly still for fifteen minutes to half an hour; continue this for three to four days or for a week until you secure full control of your physical being. Many will find this extremely difficult; others will conquer with ease, but it is absolutely essential to secure complete control of the body before you are ready to progress. Next week you will receive instructions for the next step; in the meantime you must have mastered this one.*

The books lessons, parts, or chapters do not have titles, only Part I, Part II, and so on. If I were to name this lesson, it would be called, *Be Still: Gaining Control over Your Physical Body.* How difficult can that be, I thought? Much to my surprise, sitting erect and completely still, without fidgeting was very difficult for me. It took me a while to gain control of my physical being. In fact it took me over a full year of reading, re-reading, digesting, and practicing these lessons, to feel like I understood what Haanel was writing. The depth of his message is so vast, that each time I read it I understand something differently, than before. He writes in his book that twenty or thirty years of conditioning cannot change in fifteen or twenty minutes. Believe me when I say this is the truth. We cannot undo a lifetime of conditioned thinking in one sitting, or in one year—it takes time and practice.

I am not going to share all twenty-four weeks lessons, however, the first two are what opened my mind to see my own conditioning and how it keeps me from doing what I want to do. I am honored to share these first two lessons. Should you want your own copy of *The Master Key System*, it is available from the store at www.ConnieandSheila.com.

Although each lesson contains a lot of information, I have chosen to share only the part that stood out to me. I understand what resonates with me may not be the same for you. Here is Part II of week two:

> *Last week I gave you an exercise for the purpose of securing control of the physical body; if you have accomplished this you are ready to advance. This time you will begin to control your thought. Always take the same room, the same chair, and the same position, if possible. In some cases it is not convenient to take the same room, in this case simply make the best use of such conditions as may be available. Now be perfectly still as before, but inhibit all thought; this will give you control over all thought and care, worry and fear, and will enable you to entertain only the thoughts you desire. Continue this exercise until you gain complete mastery.*
>
> *You will not be able to do this for more than a few moments at a time, but the exercise is valuable, because it will be a very practical demonstration of the great number of thoughts which are constantly trying to gain access to your mental world."*

"Inhibit thought!" Prevent thoughts from entering your mind? Was he kidding? Try it—sit and notice how long you can sit and not have a thought. This lesson was a huge challenge for me. I had never really thought about what I think about. With this lesson I was able to see how my thoughts jumped from one thing to another.

I was amazed when I began to pay attention to my thoughts. How could I have gone through life not noticing or not controlling my own mind and thoughts? In my copy of Haanel's book, I titled Part II as *Clearing the Mind Chatter*. Some people call this state of mind, "monkey-mind," with thoughts jumping from one thing to another, just like an untrained monkey jumping from one place to the next. What I mean by *THiNKING ROCKS* is we can choose what we think about. Controlled thinking leads us to a place where we can sit and completely clear our minds of all thought, like Haanel wrote, "inhibit thought." This is the place of silence. No mind chatter, no monkey-mind. This is the place where creativity happens; this is the place of God.

I believe silence is the language of God and for me to hear God; I have to be still and silent, both physically and mentally. Things are not always as they appear; power is in the silence.

Chapter 4

Balance—Mind, Body and Spirit

We become what we think: therefore a healthy mind manifests a healthy life.

~ Connie Williams

"Be sure that it is not you that is mortal, but only your body. For that man whom your outward form reveals is not yourself; the spirit is true self, not that physical figure which can be pointed out by your finger."

~ Marcus Tullius Cicero, (106BC–43BC)
Roman philosopher and orator

Deck Ten—Questioning My Beliefs

Somewhere in the middle of the Caribbean Ocean I found myself on deck ten with my partner Sheila and Steve Brickner. Steve is the husband of DeeDee, the couple who invited us on the Honduran mission trip. Both of them had become good friends of ours. DeeDee is a real estate investor and has partnered with Sheila and me on several real estate deals.

Steve is in health care and could care less about real estate, although I always admire him for the support he gives his wife in her business. We were sailing aboard a Carnival cruise ship to San Juan, Puerto Rico, Charlotte Amilee, St. Thomas, and Phillipsburg, St. Marteen during the 2009 National Real Estate Investors Association annual conference. Steve was our self-appointed guide; he didn't attend the conference classes but loved ships and cruising. We dubbed him "boat-boy." He knew every nook and cranny of that ship.

One evening while Sheila and I were having dinner with the Brickner's, Steve invited us to join him the following morning on deck ten for a morning meditation. Steve had grown up Catholic and felt he communicated better with God through meditation rather than attending mass. We met Steve the next morning on top of the ship in an area we didn't even know existed. Deck ten had a wonderfully private, yet open space where no one could see or interrupt us.

It was wonderful, sitting on the deck with the wind blowing through our hair, as we watched the bright ball of energy rise out of the ocean. We were awe struck. The beauty of nature, the wind, the water, and the morning sunrise made it easy to relax. Steve began to give us instructions on how to meditate. We enjoyed a quiet ten or fifteen minute meditation.

Even though we were in a beautiful and tranquil setting, I found it difficult to keep thoughts from racing through my mind. The thoughts thundered like the foot-falls of a cheetah chasing his prey. I decided then and there that I wasn't good at meditating. Throughout the rest of the cruise Steve shared information about energy zones in the body—things I had never heard of. He told us about chakras and the areas of our physical bodies that contain each chakra. I had never heard of chakras but was fascinated.

Steve said when we have a problem in life, it means one of the chakra is closed or blocked and the energy cannot flow. He explained that chakra is a concept used in Hinduism and Buddhism. The word chakra refers to a wheel-like vortex that is believed to exist on the surface of living beings. Chakras are said to be "force-centers" or whorls of energy that are the focal points for receiving and transmitting energies. He said some people believe there are varying numbers of chakras, but in the West the most well-known is the system of the seven chakras.

1. The Crown Chakra

2. The Third Eye Chakra

3. The Throat Chakra

4. The Heart Chakra

5. The Solar Plexus Chakra

6. The Sacral Chakra

7. The Base/Root Chakra

There is a weird feeling I get when I learn of something new. Has my life been that sheltered or is it just a cultural thing? I know meditation and chakras are not common in the West, but if using either of these systems can help a person live a more enjoyable life, why don't we use them?

When we returned from our cruise I began to research chakras and the power behind them. I wondered if this is what Charles Haanel wrote about in *The Master Key System*. I had only read his book once and it really was too far over my head for me to understand the magnitude of his lessons. I was just beginning to tap into the power of my own mind.

Each time I saw Steve he would talk about his experiences using Eastern beliefs and philosophy in his own life. I found it fascinating. He invited me and Sheila to a weekly meditation held on the campus of Vanderbilt University in Nashville. Each Wednesday evening at 5:15 p.m., Dr. Gordon Peerman and his wife Kathy Woods, led a small group of people in a guided meditation.

They have a ten or fifteen-minute opening meditation and then a thirty-minute dharma talk and close the session with another, shorter meditation. The first week on my way to the guided meditation I got lost on the campus—I knew I was going to be late. I don't advise running to a meditation, it doesn't work.

You cannot run into a place panting, then sit down and relax quickly. I learned I needed to get there a little early to give myself time to relax and quiet my mind. It took several weeks for me to get comfortable with the idea of meditating, much less meditating with a group of people. Did I tell you I was raised in a full-gospel church? We don't meditate in the Assembly of God church or any full gospel church for that matter. I guess the teaching would be an idle mind is the devil's workshop."

I'd heard that growing up, but when I decided to gain control of my own thoughts and my own mind, it occurred to me that I didn't have to abide by the teachings of my youth. Here's the reality—I was so far removed from the teachings of my youth, I often had to reconsider what I was doing. I questioned the things I was learning, but I liked the answers that came to me. I love my parents and I am thankful for the way I was raised. I have always had a strong faith and belief in God, but I found myself, as an adult, questioning those long-held beliefs.

I find some teachings of the church interesting. For example: "an idle mind is the devil's workshop." After recently researching this teaching, I ran across a comment on the internet by someone named Britney and I like what she had to say on the subject.

> *"An idle mind is the beginning of awakening. An idle mind is a quiet mind. This is the purpose of meditation, to quiet the mind and come face to face with self, your spirit. A busy mind knows no peace and never achieves awakening."*

I like Britney's way of explaining an idle mind. Each time I meditated I found myself feeling more and more connected with God. Taking the time to get still, to sit, and to be quiet is when I hear God. I believe silence is the language of God. When I am too busy, how can I ever hear God?

This sort of thinking was new for me. I had always been taught to pray and that prayer meant consciously choosing the words to say, whether praying or praising. You know when you are with someone who talks all of the time and you cannot get a word in? That is what I think we sometimes do with prayer; we talk—we never listen.

It is only when I am listening that I feel I am in real communication with the creator of the universe. When I first began meditating I felt as if I was doing something wrong. Most Christians don't commune with God in this way. Meditation is an Eastern belief.

Why are people so judgmental of other beliefs and how others commune with God? In the Concordance of the New American Standard Bible the word meditate means to ponder and the word meditation is described as deep reflection. The word, pray, it says is to ask or worship. If all we do is pray and worship, when do we ponder and reflect if meditating is not permitted?

Sometimes we believe what we do because of conditioning. I love God. I just had too many questions about the rules of the church that I was raised in, and was left with an unsettled feeling. That feeling led me to where I am now.

I cannot wrap my brain around the idea that one kind of teaching is right for everyone. We are all unique. I believe God speaks to us through different means, different people and prophets, and allows us to find our own way. What works for one may not work for others. I believe we all have to find our own way. Therefore I believe you have to THiNK for yourself.

Ask yourself what do you believe and why? Is the teaching of your youth; what you choose to believe or is your belief a result of conditioning? Many of us never question our beliefs. We live our lives, each day going through the motions but not really being plugged in.

As I began to awaken I was amazed at the power behind being "mindful." Jon Kabat-Zinn has been studying and practicing mindfulness for over thirty years. He was born in 1944 and is Professor of Medicine Emeritus and founding director of the Stress Reduction Clinic and the Center for Mindfulness in Medicine, Health Care, and Society at the University of Massachusetts Medical School. He teaches mindfulness meditation as a technique to help people cope with stress, anxiety, pain, and illness. His MBSR or Mindfulness Based Stress Reduction programs are becoming more and more popular in this country and all over the world.

Kabat-Zinn describes mindfulness more simply than anyone I have ever heard. In his book *Wherever You Go There You Are: Mindfulness Meditation in Everyday Life*, he defines mindfulness this way:

- Paying attention
- On purpose
- In the present moment
- As if your life depended on it
- Non-judgmentally

Sounds simple enough. Being mindful is simple—but not easy.

Big Mind, Small Mind

Dr. Gordon Peerman explains in his book *Blessed Relief: What Christians Can Learn from Buddhists about Suffering*, the difference between having a Big Mind and Small Mind. He defines *Big Mind* as the mind that does not split experience into dual pairs of opposites such as good/bad or right/wrong, but sees beyond conventional dualistic thinking. The *Small Mind*, Peerman says, "is for the narrow, grasping mind, reaching out whenever it can for pleasure, praise, recognition, or gain; the dualistic mind that splits experience into opposites." I had always heard of the big picture but never the Big Mind. God sees the big picture. To see a glimpse of the big picture, I must have a Big Mind, allowing each person to worship however they choose.

Having a Big Mind allows me to control my ego when it wants to tell people what to do or how to do it. Being small-minded traps us into a world where we think we are right. Once we begin to open up to see God's big picture we realize it is a great big world out there with all kinds of people, people who are entitled to their own thoughts and beliefs. When I find myself thinking with my Big Mind I am able to see beyond the conventional dualistic thinking Gordon writes about.

It is in those times that I know I am no better than anyone else. I am able to see the beauty in all things. I am able to love people, no matter who they are or what they do or say. When I feel sorry for someone, (as if I am in some way better than they are), or get irritated—I know I am being very small-minded. We are all human and we do have an ego. We sometimes oscillate between the two, being Big Minded sometimes, while other times allowing ourselves to be Small Minded. Like so many other things in our lives, we can apply The 80/20 Rule (Pareto Principle), and ask what mind are we in? There was a time in my life when I was living a twenty percent Big-Minded life and an eighty percent Small-Minded life. It isn't something I meant to do; I just didn't know I had a choice.

The twenty percent was spent on, occasionally attending church, saying bedtime prayers, praying before a meal; helping others, and wondering why people do what they do. I was judgmental, and disconnected from my spirit and more connected to the physical world. The majority of my days were not spent consciously or being in the moment, but instead mindlessly going through life. I wasn't consciously thinking, or being connected to our Creator.

Today my practice is to live an eighty-percent Big Mind life, allowing my ego to come on the scene only twenty percent of the time. We have a choice whether to be kind and loving, conscious of our thinking, living in the present moment, (Big Mind), or living a life of dread or regret, wishing life were different (Small Mind). Why wouldn't we choose the Big Mind?

These days I consider Gordon Peerman not just a wise teacher, but my friend as well. He is a psychotherapist and has been an Episcopal priest for over thirty years. Gordon has been able to weave the teachings of Jesus, Buddha, Moses, and the prophets, Muhammad, Lao Tzu and others, into his teachings in a way that makes me feel we are All One.

Gordon writes in his book that he doesn't need to give up Thich Nhat Hanh to read Matthew, Mark Luke, and John.

Moving beyond the limitations of my own Small Mind has allowed me to know and understand that we each have our own path to find. No one can tell you what is right for you. When we find the path to love; love for all beings, (including murderers), and we allow ourselves inner peace—a peace that passes all understanding, we have found the right way. Whatever brings these things into your life is what is right for you. What is right for me might be different. I believe we can both be right.

Four Noble Truths

The core of the Buddhist teaching is the Four Noble Truths: There is suffering. There is a cause to suffering. There is an end to suffering. There is a path out of suffering. One of the first things I learned about the Buddhist teaching is that we cause ourselves to suffer. We can't help it; it is part of being human, it is part of life. Sometimes we are grasping for things, wanting things to be different than they are. When we allow these desires to cause us pain, this is suffering, and it is our choice.

When I grieved for Carl, I wanted things to be different than they were. I didn't like the fact that he had been murdered, but he had been. I was arguing with reality. I hated that no one had been charged with his murder, but no one had. I was arguing with reality. I hated that I couldn't call my brother and hear his voice, but I couldn't. Not being able to call him made me sad, and I know now that I caused myself suffering because I was arguing with reality.

Carl was never going to be at a family gathering, no holidays, no birthdays, weddings, or funerals. He wouldn't be at family board game nights, or play tennis—no graduations, nothing. I was grasping, trying to hold on to something that was not ever going to be. I was causing my own suffering. We all do it. Sometimes people move through it and sometimes they don't.

My father didn't. He didn't realize there is an end to suffering. He didn't know he could change his thinking and make all the pain go away. The path out of suffering is nothing more than the way we think and what we choose to do. Are we present? Are we consciously living in the now, or, are we living in the past or future wishing things were different? Today is the day.

Being Positive

We grow up with scriptures like Philippians 4:13, "I can do all things through Christ who strengthens me." For some reason our daily lives are out of control. Maybe we believe somehow that doesn't apply to us. If we did we wouldn't go around saying things like I can't do that, or I need more money, or other words that mean my life would be so much better if this or that were different.

Our negative self-talk is what keeps us from having a phenomenal life and loving each and every day. Knowing we become what we think and that a healthy mind manifests a healthy life, why think negatively? Why not change our thoughts to those with more positive outcomes? Why are so many people living paycheck to paycheck? How are there so many people living lives they don't like? Many people are living in bad or mediocre relationships, instead of having a relationship filled with romance, love, and happiness.

You have probably heard the saying, "There is no way to happiness, but happiness is the way." That is what I am talking about, since happiness is the way, we must *think happy*. Instead we end up living lives as Thoreau said, "in quiet desperation." We think something needs to change in our life. When we shift our thinking to what we DO like, and lose the negative self-talk, good things will come.

Discovering Balance

Discovering balance between mind, body, and spirit starts in the mind. Before Jesus Christ was ever born, Tully, as he was known by his friends, and Cicero the Roman philosopher said,

> *"Be sure that it is not you that is mortal, but only your body. For that man whom your outward form reveals is not yourself; the spirit is true self, not that physical figure which can be pointed out by your finger."*

Cicero knew his true self was his Spirit. Until we get in touch with our true self, until we tap into the power of our mind and that part which connects us to God, the creator, the universe or whatever name you choose, our life cannot have balance. A lot of us think we live a balanced life, but when we long for things to be different than they are at this moment—we are out of balance.

Often times when we talk about spirit, people think of religion. It seems to me that God has no religion. We are all connected to God through our Spirit. The Greek word for spirit is pneuma—defined as breath. God breathed life into each of us and that is our spirit.

Spirit is our connection to God and we all have it. All people are connected through spirit. Spirit makes us one. It doesn't matter if we are Catholic, Baptist, Buddhists, Methodist, Church of Christ, Lutheran, Pentecostal, Hindu, Muslim, Baha'i, Presbyterian, or atheist; we are connected to God through spirit. It is who we really are.

The Greek word for soul is psyche, (mind or emotions), which comes through thought. Our thoughts and the emotions they bring are our connection to our spirit. Judgment, racism, and anger and all the other negative thoughts divide us.

The Greek word for body is soma. Soma is defined as the entire body of an organism, exclusive of the germ cells. When we look at all three, spirit, mind, and body, it is easy to see how much of a balancing act it can be.

Living a balanced life takes daily practice. I have to be present and I have to be conscious to stay connected. The challenges of our lives that throw us off balance are the very things we should learn from. It is an opportunity to grow spiritually. Challenges of the mind and the body, allow us to see if we are of a Big Mind or a Small Mind.

For a long time after Carl was murdered, I was of a Small Mind. My thoughts were very negative, which separated me from the whole. My thoughts of the murderer led me to think he was evil. I later realized he was not evil, only his actions. God breathed life into the murderer and their real being is a spiritual being that connects with my spirit being. We are one. When I hated him, I hated myself. When I wished him harm, I wished myself harm. Until my thoughts went beyond the physical and mental world, I would always think of the murderer as different.

When I got passed my body and mind and connected with my true self, I was able to genuinely love this person. This can only come from a Big Mind mentality.

Through daily practice the Big Mind shows up more, it is why I called this book thinking consciously rocks. I must be consciously aware of what I choose to think. What I feel is rooted in what I think. In turn, what I think and feel determines what I do and say.

My search for balance is an ongoing one. Although I feel I have evolved spiritually and mentally (thanks in part to writing this book), I sometimes struggle physically. My goal, now that I have found balance in my spirit and mind is to work on my body. My work requires me to sit at my computer often. My body is lacking much needed exercise and continues to be a challenge for me. I know I am going to come through this a much stronger person when I accept the body I have. However, I am still working on that part. Very seldom in the past was I ever completely happy with my body. I would beat myself up for gaining weight or not exercising.

When we think of all the things that are wrong with our bodies, we can keep ourselves in a mode of suffering. When we want things to be different than they are, we are arguing with reality.

Putting these practices to use in my current life has helped me to gain a new appreciation for my body. Now I focus on the things that I love about my body, and that brings confidence. Little by little, I am shedding my discontent and learning to love my body, which brings balance to my life.

To live a balanced life we must have balance in all three areas—mind, body and spirit. We must learn to live with a Big Mind, and not separate ourselves from others. We become what we think; therefore a healthy mind manifests a healthy life. Balance does not happen overnight, it takes daily practice.

Chapter 5

Money Follows Thoughts

"We're only poor if we think we're poor."

> *"You are today where your thoughts have brought you; you will be tomorrow where your thoughts take you."*
>
> ~ James Allen
> (1864 – 1912) British philosophical writer

"THERE is a thinking from which all things are made, and which, in its original state, permeates, penetrates, and fills the interspaces of the universe. A thought in this substance produces the thing that is imaged by the thought. Man can form things in his thought, and by impressing his thought upon formless substance can cause the thing he thinks about to be created." ~Wallace D. Wattles (1860-1911)

Wattles was an American, New Thought author, and writer of the 1910 book called *The Science of Getting Rich*, which became his best work. What I admire more than anything about this man is his encouragement to his readers to test his theories on themselves rather than take his word as an authority. He claimed to have tested his methods on himself and others before publishing them. His methods work for those who think they will.

You Are What You Think

Until the last few years, I didn't consciously think about my thoughts. Once I began to think about my thoughts I began to notice how often I worried about money, work, my weight, problems loved ones were having, the economy, global-warming, or the end of time.

In 2007 my good friend John Hickman introduced me to the Law of Attraction and Rhonda Byrne's book, *The Secret*. Reading that book made me aware of all the things I knew I didn't want in my life. What shocked me was how difficult it was for me to sit and name the things I wanted. I knew what I didn't want. For instance I knew I didn't want to be poor or be a size 12 or 14. I knew I didn't want my loved ones to suffer through problems. I didn't want to struggle with work issues or be sick. I didn't want to be sad every time I thought of my brother or my father. I didn't want, I didn't want, I didn't want. Why is it I knew what I didn't want but found it so challenging to know what I wanted? The more I read Byrne's book, the more my eyes were opened. I lived in a world of "I don't want" rather than a world of "I do want." My life was and is nothing more than the results of The Law of Attraction at work.

Through the law of attraction I was drawing illness into my life. I was rarely grateful for a healthy body. Instead my thoughts were focused on being sick and wondering what might be next. My body couldn't be healthy because my mind and my thoughts wouldn't let it. As a result of being wrong-focused, came mononucleosis, shingles, knee surgery, back surgery, hysterectomy and the list goes on. I was slowly killing myself. I was experiencing the same thing with my finances—I couldn't be rich because I was worried about money.

Through my worry and negative thinking, I was drawing into my life the very things I worried about. The car did break down, the house did need repairs, and we didn't have the money to go on vacation. My thoughts were—*we don't have enough*. The reality was we always had enough. We always had what we needed. Never once have Sheila and I been homeless, and never have we been without food or clothing. We cannot be rich with this mentality. We cannot fret about money and expect there to ever be more. We can never be rich if we think of ourselves as being poor, broke, or needing more.

Becoming an Entrepreneur

I was a child consumed with the need to have more money. The desire continued into my young adulthood. When Sheila and I met I was 21 years old and she was 24. We met in June of 1986. We spent that summer going to movies, dinner, concerts, playing putt-putt, going camping and just getting to know one another. This relationship was like no other that either of us had ever had, for a whole lot of reasons.

I learned that summer that like me, Sheila had a desire to own her own business. In February, 1987, we bought a house and started our life together. Two months later we were in business. Literally.

We quit our jobs at Opryland USA and opened C&S Retailers. There was a new open-aired mall northwest of town called Fountain Square and we sold plush animals from a cart sitting out in the courtyard. The summer of '97 was a fun time for us. We were selling the heck out of teddy bears and baby dolls, making lots of money, or so we thought. If only we didn't have to pay rent for the carts, pay for the merchandise, pay sales taxes, and keep records of everything we bought and sold, we might have survived. We didn't realize it at the time, but we were sinking fast.

When the season changed and the weather turned cold, shoppers no longer came to the open-aired mall. They went to the enclosed mall. Since we couldn't sell our children's toys where we were, we met with the manager of Rivergate Mall, northeast of Nashville. Ron, the manager, allowed us to open a kiosk in the middle of the mall. At the time kiosks were not as prominent as they are today. We were the second kiosk ever to go in Rivergate Mall. (The first kiosk, if you're wondering, sold jewelry.) We were told the oak and smoked glass kiosk we had ordered and paid $8000 for would not be ready when we opened. We knew we had to be open for "Black Friday," the biggest shopping day of the year, so we spent Thanksgiving night in 1987 setting up the temporary kiosk my father built. On Black Friday, we were back in business. The crowd was amazing. We sold a ton of merchandise so much that one of us had to run home to get more stock for the shelves.

Before we opened in our new location, Ron had us sign a 3-year, $75,000 contract with the mall management company. (Can you believe we leased 168 square feet of space in an enclosed mall for over $2000 a month in 1987?) It took a while to understand our expenses always exceeded our income.

We were young and naive, adventurous and willing to work hard. Sheila and I worked seven days a week, fourteen to eighteen hour days for nine months. In December we hired two girls part time. Sundays were the only day we allowed ourselves a break, and we couldn't afford that. The mall was only open from 1:00 p.m. – 6:00 p.m. and we paid for seven to fourteen hours of labor, depending on how busy the mall was. If it was a busy time, both girls worked, if the mall was slow, we only scheduled one person. We were exhausted; yet in denial that our business was failing. We were behind on paying our vendors and were running out of money to order more goods.

We were behind on the rent and on paying our personal bills. We simply weren't making enough money to pay our expenses. We had to sell a lot of teddy bears to make a profit large enough to cover the expenses, while still paying on the kiosk, and for Sunday labor. Our business was in big trouble. We owed a lot of people a lot of money. How could we tell them we couldn't pay them? What were we going to do?

It was May 1988, and we felt our only option was to file bankruptcy. Ron, the mall manager assured us he would let us out of the lease. We still owed two and a half years on the lease, plus the amount we were behind, a total of nearly $70,000. We owed a supplier over $1,000 for the plush animals we had already sold. We were also in debt to other vendors and the Tennessee Department of Revenue.

We had purchased our house about one year earlier and since there was no equity, the mortgage company allowed us to reaffirm and keep the house. I don't remember the dollar amount we filed on, but I think it was around $100,000. I look back now and I am amazed how hopeless we felt over $100,000 worth of debt. In those days I didn't think the way I do today about money.

Coming back from the Abyss

After attending the bankruptcy hearing and standing on the courthouse steps Sheila and I shook hands and said it was fun, it was scary, we learned a lot, but we never want to go through that again. Not long after the notification letters were mailed to the creditors we received a copy of a letter from Sam and Martha Sanders. Handwritten on the same form letter notifying them we were filing on our debt to them, were the words—"Oh to have lived and never tried. Consider this debt paid in full."

We both began to cry and couldn't believe the compassion we felt and the encouragement this gave us. When we left the retail business we got a job working for a family-owned screen-printing business. Sheila was one of two sales people and I did the artwork for the tee-shirts and hats they sold. We enjoyed the work. Sheila was on the road five days a week and great in sales. She established quite a client base. I learned a lot about graphic work cutting lithograph by hand, creating logos with India ink and clear film and using rub off letters for the company name and number.

After seeing the antiquated way I created art for the projects, a client and local business owner allowed me to come to his trophy shop once a week and set type using his new Macintosh SE. (That was 23 years ago and the beginning of my love for Macs.) I love Mac and years later when Sheila began learning about computers, she learned on a PC. We are the perfect pair for the commercial, I'm a Mac, and she's a PC.

We worked for this company for about a year and discovered the business was in financial trouble. The orders Sheila sold, were taking longer and longer to produce and deliver. Her clients were being given a delivery date of two to three weeks and it was taking five and six weeks. Because the company was behind on paying for the cost of goods on previous orders it was delaying buying merchandise for new orders. Things started to spiral out of control for this company and we didn't want to go down with it.

Even though it had only been about one year since Sheila and I had stood on the courthouse steps crying, hugging and shaking hands, saying we'll never do that again—we were about to venture into another business. We decided with our newfound talents; Sheila selling promotional products and me creating the art for company logos, we would open our own screen-printing company.

We didn't know everything about screen-printing but we knew we could learn. One former client offered to become a silent partner when Sheila told him we could not deliver his order. He was in the auto detailing business and really big into racing. He thought being a silent partner in the business could help him get his products at a discount for his racing and detailing business. We were young, naïve and desperate. He had money and we didn't. We agreed to give him fifty-one percent ownership of the business and allow him to be a "silent" partner. (Did I mention we were young, naïve and desperate?)

We rented a room in the back of a flower shop, signed a one-year lease, and we were thankful for what we had learned from the big mall contract.

Our rent was $260 each month—we had learned a thing or two about paying hefty rents. The building wasn't pretty, but it didn't have to be. Our customers never saw our operation and we didn't have to impress anyone with our building or location. They didn't come to our office because we went to theirs. This one large room was all we needed to produce the incoming orders.

We bought a 4-color manual press, a commercial dryer, and a screen exposure unit. We were fortunate enough to set up an account with a local printing supply company and two separate textile companies. We were ecstatic to get net 30-day terms with each company. We didn't have to pay for what we bought until 30 days later, giving us time to buy, produce, deliver, and collect on orders we sold.

My sister Cindy worked for the same screen-printing company where we had formerly worked. Once we got our company up and running, Cindy came to work with us. In less than one year we knew this business was not doing well. Unlike the company we previously worked for and learned from, we weren't in financial trouble, but partnership trouble. Our company was making money.

It turned out several months into our agreement, our partner was not silent, and he began taking money from our operating account to buy things for his business. We knew this was not going to work out and when we told him so, he wasn't very nice about it. Sheila and I knew we had to get out of the partnership.

About five miles down the road we learned Sam and Martha Sanders were in the beginning stages of a new start-up screen-printing company. This is the very couple that just one year earlier we had filed bankruptcy on for $800. When you have no money $800 is a lot of money. Even though we received the kind letter from them, we always knew we would pay that debt back. This couple had helped us in so many ways and now we were going to them one more time to ask for help.

We met with Sam and explained the predicament we were in with our silent partner. We were soon to be walking away from our company so we asked Sam if he would allow us to rent his printing equipment in the evenings while it was not in use. Our plans were to save enough money from our sales to buy our own equipment and start all over. I must say, looking back on this idea to start another screen-printing company was really desperate. But what else could we do? We had tried to make it on our own since quitting our jobs at Opryland. Three years is a very long time when you are trying to make something happen that just won't happen. We had started two separate businesses and neither was successful.

We thought we would make it big, make lots of money, and live the good life. We found ourselves broke and scared to death, asking what we would do if Sam said no. We never imagined that Sam would have another idea. He is a great listener and after crying on his shoulder, he made us an offer we couldn't refuse. Before you think, "Oh no, not another partner," understand this is the man who wrote on the bankruptcy notification letter, "Oh to have lived and never tried, consider this debt paid in full." This man is kind and generous; he is good, and an awesome businessman. Sam is a salesman, inventor, world traveler, free thinker, and a great husband and father. Sam taught us the win-win philosophy.

He said, "If the deal isn't good for both sides, don't do it." Renting us the equipment so we could start all over wasn't a good idea, in his opinion. They had just taken an order to print 35,000 tee-shirts with a three-color chest imprint and a one color back. In fact that is the reason they got into the printing business, to print this one order. Of course they knew there would be more to come, which is why he asked us to come onboard with him. We knew his offer meant giving up the desire to start another company of our own.

We were thrilled beyond thrilled, as long as Cindy could come along too. She had turned into a talented printer and we knew she would be as valuable to him as Sheila and I. The thought of getting an actual steady paycheck was more than we could handle. Sheila and I were both so excited; we could barely sleep that night. We hadn't had a W-2 since leaving Opryland, me in '86 and Sheila in 1987. We hadn't had a steady paycheck for almost three years.

The business grew so much we moved into a larger building, bought more equipment, and hired more labor. We were no longer just a screen-printing company, but a one stop shop. Sam and Martha's business had grown into an advertising specialty business, selling imprinted coffee mugs, calendars, ink pens, embroidered jackets and hats, etc.

Sam was importing goods from China and Taipei to sell in the US. Anything a company wanted to buy; whether printed; embroidered, stamped, engraved, or embossed we could deliver. It was in my office, at this company where I took the call from Mom in April 1994. I answered the phone and heard her say, "Honey, I think Carl may have been killed last night." It was Thursday. We buried my brother on Saturday but I didn't go back to work until Tuesday. When I went back to work, I couldn't function. My mind was spinning. How could I just pop back into my daily routine as if I had just had another ordinary weekend? This was like no other time in my life. There was nothing normal about this time. I didn't even think how this might affect Sam and Martha and our production schedule. I couldn't concentrate. I asked Sam for the week off.

Experts say you shouldn't make life-changing decisions after a personal tragedy, but within one month of Carl's murder, Sheila and I were about to open our third startup business. After I settled back into work Sam approached Sheila and I and shared what was on his heart.

He said his business had taken a direction that he really didn't want to go in and it had gotten bigger, faster than he had planned. He told us he thought Sheila and I were great. He offered to help us open our own ad specialty company. I have always admired Sam for the way he talks to people. He can fire someone and they will walk out the door thanking him.

In June 1994, we opened Nashville Advertising & Promotions, Inc., with only a computer, desk, filing cabinet and ninety percent of the profits (about $7,500) from the orders we sold in the month of May, all given to us from Sam and Martha. We had been pushed out of the nest and once again—Sheila and I were flying solo. We learned a lot about business from Sam and Martha Sanders and are grateful to this day that our paths crossed. We operated NAP from a home office until 1997, until we opened our fourth start-up.

Through NAP, we were selling a lot of embroidered goods, which we contracted out to embroidery companies. For a while we got quality work and quick turnaround times on embroidered items. As embroidered goods became more and more popular, our suppliers produced lower quality work and production slowed. We decided to open our own embroidery company to fill the orders for NAP. We first contacted our local NAP competitors and asked them if we opened an embroidery company would they feel comfortable giving us their business? We got a resounding yes from all of them. They were also having trouble getting the quality and production time they needed.

In February 1997 we rented a building close to downtown Nashville and opened E Wear Direct Embroidery. E Wear was contracted by NAP for all embroidery sales and our NAP competitors brought orders as well. The business grew very quickly and about every six months we were buying more machines.

When Garth Brooks was on his World Tour and the Dixie Chicks were at the top, we embroidered so many caps, shirts and jackets that we had to run three shifts, seven days a week. We joke that our business history has either been feast or famine.

E Wear was so busy that once again Sheila and I were working 18 hours days. But we loved it—for a while. A person can only work those hours for so long before getting burned out. We were making money, paying our bills; paying labor, supplies, rent, taxes, and equipment loans. But we weren't happy. We realized it wasn't more money that was going to make us happy. The nature of the embroidery business is "gotta have it now." There were always deadlines to meet and production was always going to be crazy busy. We were not in control of our time. We decided no amount of money was worth the way we felt. Tired and worn out we met with a commercial broker to get information on selling E Wear. We ended up selling to a local embroidery company. It took a few months of negotiating, but eventually we came to an agreement and sold E Wear.

In October 2000 we moved our NAP office from the E Wear building to our home. It was nice, just Sheila and me; no employees, and no demands from a busy industry—no huge monthly overhead and no business debt.

Working from home was a real gift. When we began planning our next move after the sale of E Wear, we knew NAP was still a viable company. We looked for a smaller building or office to rent because NAP didn't need a lot of space. We were the middleman or broker, selling and delivering promotional products. Since we couldn't find the space we were looking for, we decided to set-up an office in our house. After 11 years working out of an office in our home, we couldn't imagine having to commute to an office every day.

Three years seems to be my attention span for a business. The aftershocks from the whirlwind days of E Wear settled down. Sheila and I had revived the faint heartbeat that lay within NAP. Our days were spent selling ad specialty merchandise to companies and corporations.

We had some great accounts that ordered hundreds of thousands of dollars' worth of merchandise. We didn't have to work as hard to get orders, new accounts, or to collect money the way we did when we began NAP. Our clients paid well and we were making a steady income. NAP had been around for nine years, which included the three-years of running E Wear.

It is funny how life happens. Just when something is supposed to happen it does. Or maybe I am talking about that old saying, "When the student is ready; the teacher appears." In the fall of 2003 Sheila bought a book by Robert Kiyosaki called, *Rich Dad, Poor Dad*. She read the first few pages while standing in the bookstore and was intrigued and thought I might like the book. I had never been an avid reader, but when I did read it was non-fiction. I have always been a self-help junkie. I love it when people share motivating, inspiring, and educational stories of their life. *Rich Dad, Poor Dad* was just that.

Kiyosaki encourages his readers to become financially literate. He shares stories of his own life growing up in Hawaii where he learned from his father, "Poor Dad" and his best friend Mike's dad, whom he refers to as, "Rich Dad." His books focus on the different approaches of these two mentors. Kiyosaki shares their thinking, behaviors, and the actions they take. The sub title for the book really explains the content perfectly; the complete title is *Rich Dad, Poor Dad: What the Rich Teach Their Kids about Money That the Poor and Middle Class Do Not!*

When I read this book, it was as if my whole being absorbed it. It wasn't just a book, with words; it was as if this man was speaking directly to me. I could feel his energy, his concern, his desire to teach and his passion to educate people. Three days later I was reading Kiyosaki's next book, *The Cashflow Quadrant: Rich Dad's Guide to Financial Freedom*. What I read in this book blew my mind. In it, Kiyosaki explains that anyone who works is either in one of four categories or quadrants. The left side of the quadrant, in the top left space is the Employee (E), the bottom left is the Self-Employed (S) person, and on the top right side of the quadrant is the Business Owner (B), and in the bottom right corner of the quadrant is the Investor (I). I was feeling pretty proud of myself knowing Sheila and I fell into the right side, (the good side) in the (B) area. We were after all business owners and had been for almost ten years.

As I consumed the words of *The Cashflow Quadrant* ™ I was shocked to discover we were not Bs at all, but were Ss. Business Owners he shared can leave, take a vacation, a medical leave, and when they come back their business is still running. If a self-employed person leaves for ten days it affects the business. In our case, we were in sales. If we were not out selling caps, tee-shirts, and coffee mugs, we were not getting paid.

Our business, NAP, was about to turn ten years old. I had always heard if your company makes it five years, you have passed a hurdle. We had been excited and looking forward to NAP's ten year anniversary, but learning this new information took the wind out of our sails. We didn't know what was about to happen to us, or our business, but we owe a lot to Robert Kiyosaki. (We hope to meet him one day and personally thank him for writing the books he writes and for sharing the knowledge he has acquired over the years.)

Kiyosaki encourages people to educate themselves; read more, attend seminars and workshops, hire consultants, and invest in yourself and your financial education. That is what we did and our actions changed our future.

Within a month or so Sheila and I were attending a wealth-building seminar called Soaring with Eagles. I saw the ad in the paper several days after finishing one of Kiyosaki's books. I called the number listed, made reservations for two, and we made plans to attend.

The beginning of this chapter opens with this quote by James Allen. "You are today where your thoughts have brought you; you will be tomorrow where your thoughts take you." Sheila and I had been brought through some amazing things. We had a business where we could set our own schedules, control our time, and work as much as we wanted to. We knew what we needed to earn, but for some reason could never figure out how to make it big.

We worked hard. We were diligent in bringing NAP into the twenty-first century as a successful ad specialty company. NAP was doing more and more business each year; our sales were growing but not as much as we wanted. It was still a struggle. We worried each month, wondering if we'd have enough in sales to meet the budget. We worried about whether an order would come through and if it did, we worried about production.

We worried about vendors not having enough inventories to fill our orders. We were concerned about buyers taking another position and leaving us to build a relationship with a new buyer. Many years later, as I write this book, I look at all the worry. I noticed our thinking was not healthy at all for the growth of our business. We worried too much for our business to thrive. When I wrote earlier in this chapter that James Allen's methods work for those who think they will, I believe that with all of my heart. It has been only in the last few years that I realize you really can be RiCH—money follows thoughts.

Our thoughts weren't on the right things. We had blocked our own growth with worry—by not consciously thinking about our thoughts. What are our thoughts telling the Universe? We must pay attention to our intention and if our intention is to be rich, we have to THiNK RiCH. Worrying about money, business or anything else only draws that which we worry about into our lives.

If you want to know how to get rich, read the next chapter. This chapter is about where your thoughts can take you. Believe me when I tell you, I wouldn't trade any of the experiences Sheila and I have had. Our past businesses are what prepared us for where we are today. I never knew until recently how much my thinking blocks me from receiving all that life has to offer. Sheila and I were involved in a lot of different ventures, some made money, and some did not. Nevertheless, I always had the thought there was more. We were entitled to more. I wanted more. I'd ask myself, "How come I can't figure out how to have more?" I never imagined that I was the reason.

In 2011, Sheila and I read and recorded James Allen's bestselling book, "As a Man Thinketh.." The re-mastered audio book is available on our website at www.connieandsheilatalk.com/products/as-a-man-thinketh-audio-book/. If you don't currently read inspirational, motivational, and educational material, I encourage you to start. Reading books on personal development can change your life.

Chapter 6

Do and Be What You Love
Following Your Passion Leads to Finding Your Purpose

"You are not here merely to make a living. You are here in order to enable the world to love more amply, with greater vision, with a finer spirit of hope and achievement. You are here to enrich the world, and to impoverish yourself if you forget the errand."

~ Woodrow Wilson, (1856-1924)
28th President of the United States

Sheila used to ask me, "If our life doesn't get any better than this, isn't this good enough?" I understood what she meant, kind of. I knew I should be grateful for what we had. Healthy, happy, self-employed, and able to pay our bills—but I knew there was more to life. I wanted life to be great. No, I wanted life to be phenomenal, not just good enough. The desire to be RiCH from an early age is what I thought caused me to continue moving forward. (I later discovered that cause was something else.) With each business we started, we gained more knowledge, made a little more money and yet, that feeling that there was more, remained. I was determined to find more.

In the winter of 2003, at a wealth-building seminar called Soaring with Eagles, we met Greg and Ginny Pitts. They were real estate investors in Nashville. Over the three-day conference we spoke occasionally with Greg and Ginny. When we learned they owned over fifty investment properties, we asked if they would mentor us. We liked their warm personalities and laid back style. We decided to begin our mentorship with Greg and Ginny in January to give us time to enjoy the upcoming holidays. Over the next couple of months we got to know Greg and Ginny and in January we went to their house for our first lesson in real estate investing.

Thanks to the teachings of Dave Ramsey, Sheila and I were debt free; except for our mortgage. We had been on the cash envelope system. (Learn how to get out of debt at www.DaveRamsey.com) We had $30,000 equity in our house, and personal assets and cash. Our total net worth at that time was about $60,000. Our combined assets totaled less than $150,000, including the house. (If you have read Robert Kiyosaki, you know we can't add our house as an asset.)

Using the techniques that Greg and Ginny taught us and developing our own systems over the years, it still blows my mind what we have been able to do in less than eight years. Investing in real estate, buying properties to renovate and sell, and buying others to hold as rentals, we have been involved in nearly 100 transactions, We have chosen to keep seventy-one properties as rentals. Can you imagine how holding properties has increased our net worth?

The numbers are staggering to me. When I look back over the last eight years, I remember times of frustration and pain. Fear was a big factor and held us back at times. But through it all we have been able to amass a real estate portfolio worth millions dollars. The loan-to-value (LTV) on these properties averages sixty-eight percent, giving us a nice equity position.

In 2007, Sheila and I became full time real estate investors, while continuing to own and operate NAP. In 2009-2010, Sheila and I became REALTORS®. We thought it was time we got our license to help us in our investing business. Having our license allows us to control our schedule of seeing properties. In addition we get to make the commission from buying and selling instead of paying that money to someone else. You may not believe me when I tell you that somewhere around the three or four year mark of our investing, I started to lose focus. I love real estate but was becoming bored with it. I didn't realize I was bored until I started to slack off on my duties and look for other things to do.

I began learning about the stock market. Our friend Matt Koerlin and I took some classes together through Rich Dad Seminars. Sheila and Matt's wife Pua weren't as interested, so Matt and I partnered on the hefty tuition and attended several conferences and were mentored on swing trading, day trading, and buying and selling puts and calls. It was the first time I had ever heard of Fibonacci Numbers and Retracements or the Elliott Wave Principle.

I learned a lot, I paid a lot and I lost a lot. But did I say I learned a lot? It was so worth it. The whole experience was so educational, in so many ways. With training costs, plus losses I was out $20,000. There was a time when it would have killed me to pay out $20,000 for that lesson. Thankfully we were able to look at it for what it was, a great learning opportunity. One of the biggest things I learned is that I don't like to be tied to a computer. Even though we were trained how to set trades and forget them, I couldn't help but watch the market. It is kind of like a bad car wreck, you have to look.

I was watching MSNBC, CNN, Jim Cramer, and any show that talked about the stock market. Each morning I'd wait for the opening bell to ring so I could check the trades I set on my online trading account. If they hit, then I watched the stock to see whether I still believed in the stop I had placed, or if I needed to override the Stop? It was crazy. I was crazy. I needed to be around people. I am too social to do something I felt was isolating. I realized I was doing it for no other reason than to make money. How sick is that? I was pulling away from reality and living in a world of an opening and closing bell, buying and selling puts and calls and watching, waiting and listening for news on corporations I had invested in. It was a lonely world and I didn't like the person I was becoming. Sheila was very supportive of what I was doing, but she didn't know until about eight months later how I really felt. Just shy of one year after opening the trade account, we closed it, paying nearly $20,000 to learn I didn't like it.

I felt like I had let her down, though Sheila assured me that was not the case. The feeling of something more was still there. I wanted more and I couldn't help it. It had been a part of me since I was a little kid. Even with millions of dollars' worth of real estate—it wasn't enough. I've always heard "do what you love." I thought I loved real estate, I was passionate about it, but if I really loved it why was I bored?

Finding Your Purpose Not Just Your Passion

I do love real estate and investing in residential properties. It is something that Sheila and I are both very passionate about. At some point in all of this I realized that even though I was following my passion, I didn't understand my purpose. I began asking God and myself, "How can I be of service?" Surely there is something I can do to help people. What can I do that has meaning, value, and can help change the lives of others?"

The first stock training conference that Matt and I attended was overwhelming. I wondered if I could keep up. I had never been a great student and sitting in a classroom was not my favorite thing to do. The week before we left for the conference I told my sister I was excited but apprehensive. She had recently been diagnosed with Adult ADHD and her doctor had given her a prescription. She gave me three little pills and said, "Take these with you, break it in half and take it first thing in the morning." This was unusual for my sister. I was surprised by her offer. She told me they would help me focus. I did exactly as she suggested and took the pills. I could not believe how clear everything became. It was as if I was living a real life Claritin commercial. The fog had been peeled away and I was able to maintain focus throughout the day.

There was a lot of information being thrown at us, but it was as if I was a different person. I felt like I was in some kind of zone where learning was easy. I didn't feel drugged and there were no noticeable side effects from the pill. It was amazing, so amazing that I was able to study into the evening after we returned from dinner. A week after I got home, I noticed I was having problems concentrating on the very things I had done at the conference. I didn't understand why it made so much sense the week before, but now I was struggling. I called Matt. He helped me through some trades. Eventually I went to see my doctor and told him what I had experienced. Over the years he has given me many prescriptions, I didn't think this time would be any different. He told me, "I can't just give you a script for Adderall. It is an amphetamine and besides you have to be diagnosed with ADHD before I would ever give you that." I told him my sister had recently been diagnosed with ADHD and I thought I might have it too. Never in my life had I thought I had ADD/ADHD. Knowing how my sister's medication helped me, made me think I might also have ADHD.

The doctor asked me a lot of questions and afterward said, "Okay, maybe we should have you tested. If you have ADD or ADHD, I will prescribe some type of medication. A week later I was sitting in another doctor's office taking crazy weird mind tests. At the end of all the tests, it was determined; I do in fact have ADHD. Attention-Defective/Hyperactivity Disorder is typically a diagnosis for children.

When I was a child in school, children with ADD/ADHD were called goof ups, slackers, or kids not applying themselves. No one understood the disorder. The chemical messenger's in the brain of a person with ADD/ADHD don't interact with the nervous system like they are supposed to. Think of lost mail. Every now and then, no matter how good the US Postal Service is, mail gets lost. My brain is like a bad postman—who can't get every piece of mail delivered. In the voice of Jerry Seinfeld, I call my brain Newman. What I have learned about ADHD through a support group that Sheila and I attend twice a month is that when you meet a person with ADD or ADHD, you have met one person with ADD/ADHD. It doesn't manifest the same in all people.

I also learned the hyperactivity doesn't mean hyper like, over active or can't sit still. It means hyper, as in too high or too much activity, like in hypertension, or high blood pressure. I tend to have too many projects or tasks going on at one time. It is the way my brain works. I have to consciously be aware of what I am putting on my to-do list. What I want to get done versus what I can actually complete. Hyper-focus is another side effect of ADHD. For me, that part is good and bad. In fact I think overall having ADHD can be a good thing.

When I started taking medication for ADHD it was like the fog rolled away. I had a sense of clarity I had never had before. I could focus better and pay closer attention to what I was doing—this new state of being amazed me. There I was in my mid-forties finally realizing my true potential. Sheila and I had successfully started a real estate investing company and although I do think we provide a wonderful service, something inside of me was still missing. When we buy a crappy house and fix it up so someone would want to rent it; it makes us feel good. We help neighborhoods by making the ugly house and yard more attractive, which in turn helps increase the property values.

In the first few years of our investing career, we were able to increase our net worth dramatically. But you cannot buy groceries with equity. The need for money was still there. I thought we needed to be more liquid, even though I loved owning all the rental property. I also wanted to have more cash in the bank. It's all a part of that desire to be RiCH.

It wasn't long after I started the stock training when I answered the call to write this book. I am not sure if the medication for ADHD had anything to do with my ability to sit calmly and put my thoughts on paper or not, but it has been through the writing of this book that I have found my purpose.

The Right to be Rich

Some time ago I asked God, "How may I be of service?" I know now I could never reach the level of service I wanted, until I changed the way I thought. I believe God has a plan for me. In the opening chapter of *The Science of Getting Rich*, Wallace Wattles writes,

> *"Whatever may be said in praise of poverty, the fact remains that it is not possible to live a really complete*

or successful life unless one is rich. No man can rise to his greatest possible height in talent or soul development unless he has plenty of money; for to unfold the soul and develop talent he must have many things to use, and he cannot have these things unless he has money to buy them with."

Later in the same chapter Wallace writes,

"Man's right to life means his right to have the free and unrestricted use of all the things which may be necessary to his fullest mental, spiritual, and physical unfoldment; or in other words, his right to be rich."

We have the right to be rich, happy, and successful, and living the life we dream of. It is our birthright to have these things. As God's children we all have the right to live phenomenal lives, but our thinking keeps us from living that life. Instead of thinking of wealth, living in abundance, and having all the money we'd ever need; we instead think of how little money we have. We worry about how to pay the bills. This way of thinking is drawing scarcity into our lives. I did that for years. With all the businesses Sheila and I have been involved in, I always worried about money. The year I started writing this book, and consciously being aware of my thoughts, was the year that changed my finances.

Stop Worrying—Start Living

Sheila and I owned millions of dollars' worth of real estate, but weren't selling enough houses on the retail market to generate enough operating capital to pay our expenses. I had had it, and told her I was no longer going to worry about money. It is what I had done all my life and somehow all my life I made it through whatever financial struggle we had. We never wound up homeless; we had food and shelter, so in my mind I reasoned we would always have enough. "Quit worrying," I told myself. (A month or so earlier we had discovered while reviewing our finances that we needed an additional $80,000 for the year to make budget.) Oddly enough, we quit worrying and did what we do. We focused on our work, bought and rehabbed houses, and enjoyed our lives. We thought positive thoughts and things started to happen for us. Houses started to sell. Money started coming from places we never thought possible. I stopped worrying about money.

We started coaching new investors and received an income for that. Checks came in the mail, a few hundred here or there for utility refunds or insurance overpayments. It was awesome. When it came time to see if we had plugged the $80,000 hole, we were in awe when we realized not only did we plug the hole, we surpassed our goal. We needed $80,000 and wound up with $124,000.

When we stopped worrying about money and focused our attention on what we loved doing and took action, we made forty-four thousand dollars more than we needed. For this reason I cannot stress how important it is to choose a vocation that you love and are passionate about. The Chinese thinker and social philosopher Confucius said, "Choose a job you love, and you'll never have to work a day in your life." Buddha said, "Your work is to discover your world and then with all your heart give yourself to it." We have to be our best, and the only way we can totally give our best is when we are passionate about what we choose to do for a living.

My friend Dan Miller is an expert at this. Not only in his life, but in helping others uncover their dreams and passions. Dan asks, "What does it mean to be fully alive in your work? Many of us are not yet doing what God put us here to do."

Dan Miller is the author of the widely acclaimed *48 Days to The Work You Love* and *No More Dreaded Mondays*. I love

Dan and his message that life is what we make it. Life doesn't have to be lived where we shout TGIF on Fridays and on Sunday begin to dread Monday. Sheila and I, many years ago used to joke that we might change our tag line for our business to "NAP—where every day is Friday." (Instead we chose to keep our tag line of, "Think Big, Dream Bigger") That is the way we live life. We don't dread any day of the week, nor do we celebrate one day over the other. For more info on transforming your life and career, you can find Dan Miller at www.48Days.com.

Charting Your Course

Let me tell you a story about a chicken. This chicken lived on a sailboat. This was no ordinary chicken. Well maybe the fact that it was a white chicken made it kind of common, but everything else about it was extraordinary. Can you picture it, a white chicken on a sailboat? Crazy, I know; but this chicken taught me something that I feel the need to share.

In the spring of 2009 Sheila and I began taking sailing lessons. Neither of us had ever owned a boat or was familiar with watercraft. But there was something magical about the idea of sailing that made us want to learn to sail. We dreamed of being on the lake as the sun goes down and seeing the reflection of the setting sun, or running across the water—a golden path leading from one shore to the other. I think of that picture and see God's watercolor painting. Just thinking about it makes me pause and take a deep breath.

We had only been sailing a couple of times, once while vacationing in Seattle and another time in Nashville. Each time we were left with the feeling of wanting to sail more. Before we ventured out to buy a sailboat we thought it best if we knew how to sail. Novel idea, don't you think? The spring and summer of 2009, most every Wednesday afternoon you could find us on Percy Priest Lake. We found a lovely couple at a local yacht club and asked them to teach us the basics of sailing.

We wanted to buy a boat and feel confident that we could actually sail her.

Bob and Kathy, a couple that loves sailing more than eating, mentored us. Did I mention we had no prior experience sailing, nothing nautical, or boating? The first mistake we made as we stepped onto the vessel was calling the "sheets" ropes. Who knew there were no ropes on a sailboat? There was a whole new lexicon to sailing. We were about to become bilingual and we didn't even know it. Our first language was English, our second—sailing.

As the weeks turned into months we began to speak sailing rather well or at least I thought so. My nautical vocabulary prior to these lessons consisted only of bow, aft, port, and starboard. Although before these lessons I often got directional words mixed up. Years ago someone told me that when you aren't sure which port is or starboard, remember that P-O-R-T has four letters like L-E-F-T. Oh, so portside is on the left side, got it!

As we began to learn the difference between a jib sail and a main sail or how to use the telltales, we were proud of ourselves. We began to understand what purpose the shroud and the spreader served, and how the sails and keel actually work with the wind to propel the boat forward. We began to understand the clew and tack, the jib, and how to attach it to the halyard—why always watching your head while the boom is live became clear to us.

We were feeling pretty good about what we had learned over the past couple of months. When Bob or Kathy asked which side was the leeward side of the boat—we knew. We knew what side was windward, we knew while sitting at the helm we could control the rudder/tiller, and we knew when it was time to trim, tack or jibe. Having spent numerous hours each month on the lake, week after week learning this new language and understanding that from one sailor to the next, not all terms are the same. Sometimes we learned there were multiple names for parts of a sailboat. I felt like a complete idiot one afternoon when the biggest lesson of my sailing life occurred.

While sitting at the helm, the tiller in one hand, and the main sail sheet in the other, I looked at the chicken. Remember the chicken, the white chicken on the sailboat? Bob and Kathy, as do many sailors refer to the wind directional sitting atop the mast as a chicken. The chicken indicates the direction of the wind, which is the same as the windward side. I saw the wind shift, (because the chicken moved from pointing east to west), I shouted, (I was at this time the captain of this vessel) to my first mate, "Ready to tack (turn)?"

Bob looked at me funny and asked, "What are you doing?"

"I am tacking. "

"I know that but why?"

"The wind changed, I saw the chicken spin from one side to the other."

"Oooookkkkk, but what is your heading?"

"What do you mean?"

With a little more volume Bob asked, "What is your heading, where are you going?" And as my head cocked to one side and I obviously had a dumb look on my face, Bob asked one last time, "What is your heading, where are you going?"

All of the sudden it was like a bolt of lightning hit me, my brain clicked in. All of the teaching, all the terms, the lessons had all merged and it was clear to me what Bob was asking.

With as much excitement as I could muster through my shock of awareness I said, "I have to have a heading." I looked at Sheila who was controlling the jib sail at the time and through a lot of laughter I said, "Sheila, we have to have a heading!" It was an epiphany, or as Oprah would say, "It was my aha-moment."

There are universal laws in force in all of our lives. Whether you believe in those forces doesn't change the fact that they are still working in your life. The journey of life cannot be changed regarding moving from birth to death. No matter what we try to do we're all born and we will all die. What we must know is that we must abide by certain laws while creating this wonderful life.

There are universal laws that control most everything about life. These laws are not debatable. No one would argue Newton's Law of Universal Gravitation, more commonly known as the law of gravity. We don't have to believe in gravity for it to be present in our lives. Just as the law of gravity is at work in our lives, so are other universal laws. Our thoughts are powerful. Simply stated, if you want to change your life, you have to change your thoughts.

> *"You are not here merely to make a living. You are here to enable the world to love more amply, with greater vision, with a finer spirit of hope and achievement. You are here to enrich the world, and to impoverish yourself if you forget the errand."*
> ~ Woodrow Wilson

We have to find work we are passionate about and help others do the same. By living life this way, not only do riches come, but total prosperity. Our lives are complete and balanced in all areas. This feeling of completeness came to me when I stopped thinking that money or being rich could make me happy. Being happy doesn't mean everything in life is perfect, it just means we can look beyond the imperfections. We cannot let the things of this world determine whether we are happy. The Vietnamese Buddhist monk, Thich Nhat Hanh says, "Happiness is the way."

Life isn't about making money and getting rich; life is about serving others. When we serve others, encouraging each other to find our passion and purpose—when we show up every day and give the world our best, we get paid for it in ways we never could have imagined.

If you want to be rich, you have to THiNK RICH. If you want to serve others, think big and dream bigger. You are part of the change this world needs. You are here to enrich the world.

You may know Stephen Covey from his book *The 7 Habits of Highly Effective People.* In his book *The 8th Habit: From Effectiveness to Greatness,* Covey explains that the crucial challenge for all of us is to find our own voice and inspire others to find theirs. You have a story. You have a message others need to hear. You can help change the world.

Vincennes, IN 1966, my siblings & me in birth order
Back row R-L: Mike, Cindy, Mark
Front row R-L, Cheryl, Carl & me

Dad & me in 1966 in Vincennes, Indiana

Carl & me in 1966 in Vincennes, Indiana
(Carl's 1ˢᵗ day of kindergarten)

Me & Carl and our dog Tiny in Nashville, Tennessee 1976

Carl M. Williams, December 7, 1961 ~ April 20, 1994

Sheila & me at our 15th year Anniversary Party
Nashville, Tennessee, September 13, 2001

Sheila & me 1ˢᵗ Real Estate Investors Cruise
Grand Cayman Island, February 2005

Greg Harris, Sheila, & me, Chris Mathe: 1ˢᵗ Renovation
after being mentored by Greg & Ginny Pitts.
Nashville, Tennessee, August 2005

My family gathered in 2007 for my mother's 70th birthday. (My nephew Jon Michael was stationed in Korea serving in the U.S. Army. He is the only one not pictured.) Back row: brother's Mike & Mark, Sandi, Lisa; 4th row: Dee, Cassie, Autumn, Ashley, Jacob & Eric; 3rd row: Ciara, Carly, Jennifer, Courtney, Lauren, Kaylyn, Jordon, Garrett & Wesley; 2nd row: sister Cheryl, Chas, Mom holding Baylie, Carl Hunt, sister Cindy, and Brianna; 1st row: me and Sheila

2008 REI Cruise ~ Limon, Costa Rica; me & Sheila, Greg & Ginny Pitts, DeeDee & Steve Brickner

Honduran Mission Trip ~ July 2008 with West End United Methodist Church visiting the Heifer Office in downtown Tegucigalpa, Honduras; Front row: Fred Wilhem & Sheila Tidwell; Second row: Lauren, Beth Howard, Steve & Dee Brickner, me; Back row: Bob Howard, Phyllis & Ray Sells, Michele, Casey Reed, Dr. Trey Harrell

September 2008 Kentucky ~ Some members of The Forever Group visit Virginia Trimble-Ritter Front row: Amy Griffith (director of VIP), me, Sheila, Gail Chilton; Second row: Steve Dawson, Anna White; Third row: Frank Ritter, Verna Wyatt; Back row: Virginia Trimble-Ritter

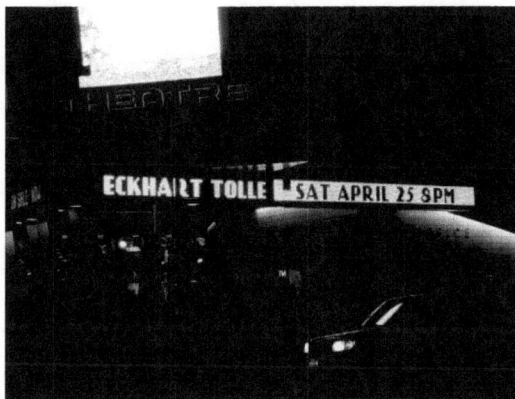

April 25, 2009 ~ Phoenix

Eckhart Tolle spoke one time in North America in 2009. He was in Phoenix and it was Sheila's 47th birthday. We went to hear Tolle and took my great niece Ciara with us.

April 2009 ~ me, Sheila and Ciara, riding the rail in Phoenix

August 2009 Birthday ~ Hang gliding in Georgia.
Breanna Bell, Melissa Crim, Sheila & me
Sheila occasionally plans air-themed birthdays for me.
Skydiving, ballooning, hang gliding, or flying lessons.
I am one day older than our friend Breanna Bell.
Our friend Melissa Crim's birthday is in August as well.

Speaking at ASTR ~ December 10, 2009
From left: Nashville's District Attorney General Torry
Johnson, MNPD Chief Ronal Serpas, and US Attorney for the
Middle District of Tennessee Ed Yarbrough, and me

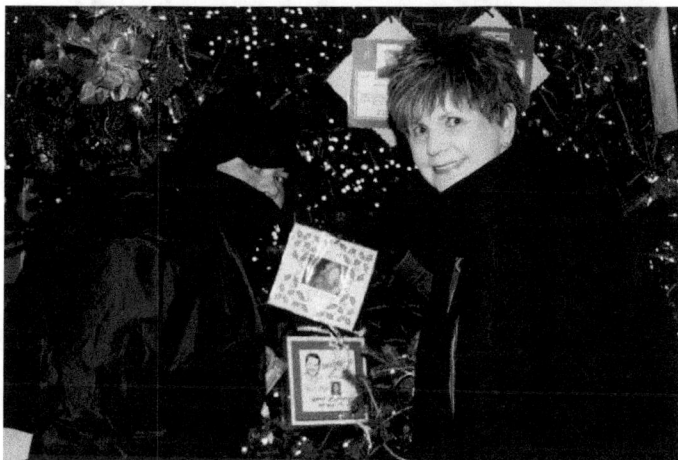

2009 ~ ASTR, Nashville, TN
Autumn Ringelstein, my niece & Mary Williams, my mother.
Both hung an ornament on the tree in memory of Carl.

February 2010 REI Cruise ~ San Juan, St. Lucia, St. Kitts
Partners meeting, me, DeeDee & Steve Brickner,
Greg & Ginny Pitts & Sheila

May 2010 ~ After the Nashville, Tennessee Floods this screech owl spent two nights in a tree in our back yard.
He is the inspriation of p.e.ACE

Not sure why Ace wears a beret, other than it makes him look cool.

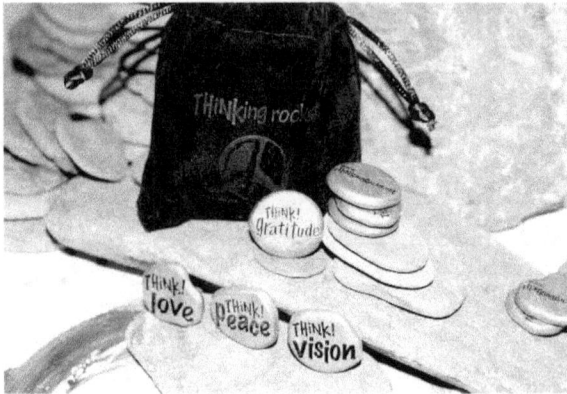

June 2010 ~ THiNKING ROCKS:
THiNK gratitude, THiNK peace, THiNK love, THiNK vision

June 2010 Connie and Sheila Talk podcast/online radio show on iTunes & at www.ConnieandSheilaTalk.com. Our friends and fellow real estate investors; Greg Self in hat, John Hickman, Sheila Tidwell and me recording episode ten titled:

"Finding Balance in Life & Business"

August 10, 2010 ~ Percy Priest Lake, Nashville, Tennessee
Sheila took me on a birthday morning sail

November 2010 ~ Nashville, Tennessee: Former Mayor of Nashville and, former Governor of Tennessee, Phil Bredesen. I'm in the middle, with former First Lady of Tennessee & founder of You Have the Power, Inc., Andrea Conte.

November 2010 Tidwell Family Trip
Gatlinburg, TN ~ Smoky Mountains
Sheila and me at the mountain chalet

Equity Mentor Group (Real Estate Investors)
2010 Christmas Party
at the home of Sher Powers and Arden von Haeger.
Sher was our REALTOR® for five years
before Sheila and I got our license.

From top: Holly Neumaier, John Hickman, Trish Simpson, Trish Vaughn, Joe & Terri Barton, Brent Bale, Deirdre & Ryan Arnette, DeeDee Brickner, Carolyn Head, David Head, Elin Stromberg, Pat & Lois Mickler, Jen & Britt Grimsley, Ginny Pitts, Linda & Richard Wofford, David & Sarah Lakey, Josh Turner, Bill Simpson, Jim Neumaier, Christopher Holl (Greg & Ginny Pitt's exchange student), me, Greg Pitts, Sheila, Chris Head, Arden von Haeger & Sher Powers.

Sheila and me
Our 25th year anniversary ~ September 13, 2011
At sea near Cozumel, Mexico

Chapter 7

Success and Significance
Stuff! How much do we need & why do we want it?

"The significance of a man is not in what he attains, but rather what he longs to attain."

~ Kahlil Gibran,
(1883 - 1931) Lebanese Artist, Poet & Writer

We live in a time where we have become obsessed with being successful. We teach our children to go to school and make good grades, so they can then go to college and get a degree, which in turn is supposed to help them get a great job. In my opinion we are training people to be worker bees, in search of the big paycheck. We ask our children, "What do you want to be when you grow up?" When they say, "I want to be fireman", "a teacher", "a policeman" or any average income-earning job, we say, "No, you want to be a doctor, or a lawyer so you can make lots of money." We have been brainwashed into thinking that making lots of money equates to being successful.

When my niece Jennifer was little she would say she wanted to be a penguin when she grew up. I am sure I squashed her dreams of ever becoming a penguin, when I told her, "I am sorry honey, and you'll never be a penguin." How did I know that? What gave me the right to squash her dream? She may have grown up to be a mascot, or work for our local NBC channel as Snowbird; the penguin who announces when schools are out for a snow day. Did I really think she would continue to want to be a penguin as she matured? By me telling her she should grow up and become a lawyer, I am perpetuating the notion that making lots of money means one is successful.

What if I had instead embraced her creativity, encouraged her to think outside of the box? At the time I was brainwashed—I believed that success was defined by money. Thinking the more money we have, the more toys we get to buy, right? You might have heard that saying, "He with the most toys in the end wins." If we have lived our lives fully, it doesn't matter how many toys we have in the end.

Connie and Sheila Talk

In March 2010, Sheila and I started a podcast. This weekly online radio show is called *Connie and Sheila Talk: Real Life, Real Estate, Real Fun*! Each Wednesday a new episode is available on iTunes and on our website at www.ConnieandSheilaTalk.com. One of my all-time favorite shows is episode 077, titled *Success or Significance*. In the October 2011 issue of *Success Magazine*, the editorial director, Darren Hardy posed a thought provoking question. He asked, "Are you living your life in pursuit of success or significance?" That got me thinking about what we do at *Connie and Sheila*

Talk as well as in our real estate businesses. As Darren Hardy notes, "You can be successful but not significant, but you cannot be significant without being successful."

Until the last few years, I shamefully have to admit I thought more about success than being significant. But in the last several years my goals have changed. Both Sheila and I want to live lives that are meaningful and significant. We want to help others pursue their dreams; just as so many have helped us get to where we are. We want to encourage and inspire people so they know they have the power to become successful and significant, not just financially, but in all areas of life—including mind, body and spirit.

What good is success, if you are miserable? If you are stuck in grief after the loss of a loved one, or the loss of a relationship, if you feel like the little depressed bubble guy on the anti-depression medication commercials, I am here to tell you—changing your thinking will make all the difference. When we change our thinking, we change our life. It isn't a quick fix. Life simply doesn't get easier overnight. It takes time. This is why it's so important to live in the Now, not worrying about the future, or regretting the past.

Understanding that our thoughts create our reality takes time to absorb. Day by day, with each new positive thought, awareness comes. Little by little we begin to see things differently. As we move from a Small-Mind, believing we are right and they are wrong, into a Big-Mind, where we live and think on purpose, in the present moment, thinking non-judgmentally, we begin to lose the suffering and life is not as complicated.

When I went skydiving, it actually felt like my brain was still in the plane as my body fell toward earth, I was disoriented. I had the same feeling when I tried to understand how my thinking caused the pain in my life. A very disorienting, feeling came over me. My head felt like it had rocks in it. I'd ask myself, Are *my thoughts keeping me from living the life I want to live?* As I began to shift my thoughts from Small-Mind to Big-Mind, and pay more attention to what I was thinking, I began to notice how often I was not present. I noticed how often I judged others. I noticed how erratic my thoughts could be. I began paying attention to what thoughts made me feel bad and what thoughts made me feel good. I began to understand that I had the power to control negative thoughts. Now I choose to think consciously, one thought at a time.

Being conscious, aware, and present seemed to open up another world. I liked living in the moment.

The Same But Different

One summer day in 2009 Sheila and I spent a Sunday afternoon at Two River's Wave Pool. Sun bathing and reading was my agenda. As I relaxed face down, on a chaise lounge, holding a book in my hands, out of my peripheral vision I noticed something hopping. I looked up and noticed a young man on all fours, lunging his body forward as his hind end rose. He was making his way to the giant slides. His mouth was wide open with a drool of spit in a constant stream. His arms were well defined but his legs were small and curled up under him.

I saw his family setting up chairs and umbrellas. A wheelchair was shaded by one of their colorful umbrellas. When they noticed he had hopped away, they called for him to come back. He looked at them, then I caught his eye and he made his way back to their camp.

As he sat in the grass, drooling and staring at nothing, I thought that although, his body may not work like mine, we are one in the same. I am no different. When our eyes met I wondered what his spirit looked like. For about 30 seconds we talked through our eyes. I broke the stare, went back to reading and in about fifteen seconds, I felt a weight drop on my back. At first I didn't realize what had happened, I heard a woman screaming. I looked up to see a young woman pulling this young man off of me.

She was mortified. His name was Junior, and she was his sister. She said he had never done anything like that before.

"I don't know why he came over here and fell on you, I guess he likes you, I am so sorry," she said.

"Really, it's OK," I said.

As she pulled him off of my back he hopped around and took hold of my feet and was leaning into them, like he was hugging my feet. His sister said, "He really likes you, I have never seen him do anything like this."

On the way home I told Sheila what had happened when Junior first got to the pool. How our eyes met, and I shared with her my thoughts about Junior being the "same but different." Our spirits were communicating through the locked gaze we shared. I think Junior wanted to let me know he heard what I was thinking. Since he couldn't speak or walk over and introduce himself, he came and fell on me. Once I absorbed what had happened, believing he had heard my thoughts, I was excited. It was cool. For the rest of the afternoon I was living in the Now.

Stories like Junior's are more and more common these days. When I am present, when I show up each day for life, amazing things happen. I learn so much. I understand now why I had such a difficult time writing this book in the beginning. I was writing from my head and not from my heart. I was trying to tell people; how to deal with and overcome grief. I wanted people to know that life doesn't have to suck. I wanted to tell people that everyone could live in abundance without worrying about not having enough. But first I had to believe it, practice it, and live it. I had to make my life amazing. I had to learn to lose my judging mind. I had to mend my relationship with Sheila, and I had to love all things—even murderers or boys who drool. My awakening felt much like a birthing process.

In humans, birth normally occurs at a gestational age of about forty weeks. Whatever happened to Junior during that time affected him physically, but not spiritually. He was as spiritually developed as I was. It took me two years to wake-up spiritually. Even after I heard the message, *"you need to quit telling people what to do,"* I was still trying to tell people what to do. I am happy to say now that I have finally learned that lesson. I very rarely allow the words, ought to, or should, or shouldn't come out of my mouth. Now I can stop myself from saying things I shouldn't say before I say them. Practicing mindfulness has allowed me to be more *present* and less judging, accepting reality for what it is.

Defining Success & Significance

I have been successful, as society defines success. I even look at the unsuccessful businesses that came first, as being successful. They taught Sheila and me what not to do, and how to do things better the next time. I love Mary Kay Ash's line, "We fall forward to succeed." There is nothing wrong in wanting to be significant. One can be successful and not significant, but one cannot be significant without being successful. Knowing this has allowed me to follow a new path. One in which I will always share the message of *THiNKING CONSCIOUSLY ROCKS*—it is the process I went through to find my purpose in life.

We have all asked ourselves about the purpose of life. In my mind the reason we are here is to love one another, enjoy life, and be happy every day. J.B. Glossinger of MorningCoach.com says "We are here for eighty or ninety years if we are lucky.

Let's make each day phenomenal, while we are on this journey."

Asking Better Questions

Significance began to unfold for me with these questions. *What is it with you and money? How much do you need? What are you going to do with all of it when you get it?* These questions make me think about money and success in a whole new way. There was a time in my life when I associated having more with being successful. I truly believed I would be happier with the things that money could buy. What I know now is that when we think things, people, or a job can bring us happiness, we will always be searching for happiness. I love Wayne Dyer and his message; "There is no way to happiness. Happiness is the way." Being happy doesn't mean everything is perfect; being happy is choosing to see beyond the imperfections of life.

When we get in touch with our true-self, when we realize we have everything we need and when we tap into the power within, we discover we don't need stuff. In an instant—happiness shines through. We lose the want for things. Peace is what we are seeking when we buy things. We believe things will make us happy and if we are happy, we can be at peace. It doesn't work that way. Have you heard the saying, "Happiness is an inside job?" So are peace, love, and joy. So are turmoil, hate, sadness, poverty, and disease. Our lives manifest from what we think. If we think we won't be happy until we get there, we'll never be happy. We have to go from there to here, from the outer to the inner, and from the future to the present.

As J.B. Glossinger says, "We are the miracle of birth." It is our birthright to have abundance. I think God intended that we have all that we want. Life is like a buffet, go get whatever you want and as much as you want. The key to happiness is losing the feeling of needing it to be happy. It's okay to want more. Desire is what moves us forward in life. As long as the desire for more doesn't leave you feeling like your life is incomplete.

Contentment comes from the inside, being present and connected to God and all things. As soon as we disconnect from being *present*, or wish for more so we can be happy, challenges will show up in our lives. Most humans don't like challenges, but as we deal with life's obstacles, we are sure to grow and mature. As we grow and share the lessons learned, success comes, but more importantly, significance comes as well.

After eight years of being real estate investors, in 2011 Sheila and I began developing our *THiNK Real Estate; Grow RiCH* product line. Our first product was *"Our First 15 Deals; A Look at Finding, Purchasing & Renovating Residential Real Estate."* We offer it for sale on our podcast website at www.ConnieandSheilaTalk.com.

The current national real estate market is not going well for most homeowners. Foreclosures are at an all-time high, property values have dropped and people are finding themselves in houses where they owe more than the property is worth. People find themselves in this market with a house they cannot sell. We have had many people call us asking for our help with these problem properties. Many of them have rented the house because they couldn't sell it for what they needed. Being a landlord is a turn-off to most people. You hear horror stories about the tenant from hell—the one who got six months behind on rent and trashed the house. I have seen it. Piles of trash filled with maggots. Maggots in the sink and fridge. Deep scratches in the hardwood floors and carpets with crayons and oil stains. Oh yeah, and big holes in the drywall, it looks like someone shot cannonballs through the walls. How does this kind of stuff happen?

Let it be known for the record that Rare Earth Properties, (our company) is the greatest landlord in Nashville. Okay, I know that is a little biased, but Sheila Tidwell makes us look great. Our tenants love us and we love them. They work hard and pay the rent on time. Many of our tenants treat our houses like their homes, because that's what we tell them. "Treat it like it's yours," we say.

We have talked to many people who have nightmarish tales. Due to our success with rental property we wrote a program titled *Landlord by Default.* We sell this program on our website to help homeowners who are contemplating renting their home. Before anyone rents a property they need the proper forms; an application to process a criminal and credit background check, a professional lease, written minimum standards, rules and regulations, and all the documents needed to protect the property owner. Being a professional landlord and renting the right way will help you get the best renter possible. Real estate is a great investment—if you do it right.

Over the years Sheila and I have been asked by many people to mentor them, and teach them the ins and outs of real estate investing. Although we did work as field coaches with some of Greg and Ginny Pitts' students, we had never mentored anyone.

In October 2011, Nathan invited us for coffee. This young husband and father of two said he was planning for the future of his family. His excitement about becoming a real estate investor was palpable. The energy from this young man reminded Sheila and me of us in our early days. We told him to give us a day, let us sleep on it, and we'd call him the next day. Because of Nathan we now have *THiNK Real Estate; Grow RiCH: Connie & Sheila's Success Guide to Real Estate Investing.* A ten-week course; outlined with lessons in the classroom and in the field. We love coaching people who are excited about real estate and the potential wealth building ability it offers.

When we began teaching others how to do what we do, instead of only being a student of real estate, significance made its appearance. It is far more fulfilling being significant to others, than creating only success for yourselves. Zig Ziglar said, "If you can dream it, then you can achieve it. You will get all you want in life if you help enough other people get what they want." The really cool thing is we don't have to wait to get all that stuff we want to be happy. Happiness is the way... to success and significance. Success isn't defined by how much stuff we have. Significance can only be defined by how much we serve others. I enjoy being significant in the lives of others far more than I enjoy success and the things money can buy.

Chapter 8

Our Minds Need Rest

Peace is not the absence of conflict, but the ability to cope with it

"A quiet mind cureth all."

~ Robert Burton
(1577-1640) English writer and clergyman

A Season to Remember

My brother Carl was 32 years old when he was murdered in April 1994. My family spent December 7th that year at the cemetery releasing helium balloons instead of getting together for what would have been his 33rd birthday. Birthdays, death dates, holidays and any day are difficult to get through after losing a loved one. In the very beginning stages of grief we carry a lot of pain that we don't know how to deal with.

The following year on Carl's birthday my Mother and I were standing in then Mayor Phil Bredesen's office at the Davidson County Courthouse. What would have been Carl's 34th birthday was the same day as *A Season to Remember*, an event the hosted by the Mayor of Nashville. "The devastation of losing a family member to violent crime can become even more difficult to bear during the holidays," Andrea Conte said. '*A Season to Remember*' is one way for families to seek healing and fellowship by coming together in remembrance of the people they love, and in celebration of the lives they led." Andrea Conte is the wife of Phil Bredesen, Nashville's 66th Mayor. He served from 1991-1999 as Mayor and then as the 48th Governor of Tennessee, serving two terms from January 2003 to January 2011.

Years earlier, the same day my brother turned 27, on December 7, 1988 Andrea Conte was kidnapped and injured in the parking lot of a retail shop in Nashville. She fought and was able to escape the kidnapper's car as it drove on the road. The kidnapper was not identified or captured immediately. The following year, he killed a woman in a Nashville park and was later captured. Under questioning, he admitted to the Conte kidnapping as well.

Following her experience, Ms. Conte founded a non-profit organization called *You Have the Power, Inc.,* (YHTP) to advocate for victims in dealing with the criminal justice system, for victims' rights, and to educate the community to prevent violent crimes. I imagine having experienced such horror in her own life led Andrea Conte to start YHTP. She and her husband care about people and especially people who are in a blurred daze from having been a victim of crime. I am thankful for both of them and the work they did when in office and for the work they continue to do.

Each year since December 7, 1995 I have attended *A Season to Remember*. It is a time where family and friends of homicide victims can gather, hang an ornament on a tree in remembrance, read their loved ones name aloud and be surrounded   by   people   who   understand.

Each year at *A Season to Remember* there is a speaker. They share their story about their loved one who was murdered. The sad thing is, each year this ceremony seems to have more and more people in attendance.

In 2009 I was asked to speak at the ceremony that was hosted by Mayor Bill Purcell. I have often said if violent crime has to happen to your family, Nashville is a great place to have it happen. People who hold high ranking positions seem to really care about victims and victim's rights. The night I spoke, not only was Mayor Purcell there, but also Chief Ronal Serpas; the chief of the Metropolitan Nashville Police Department and two deputy chiefs, Nashville's District Attorney General Tori Johnson and two assistant DA's.

U.S. Attorney for the Middle District of Tennessee Ed Yarbrough was there with two victim liaisons from his office. Amy Griffith, director of the *Victim Intervention Program* of the Metropolitan Nashville Police Department and two counselors from her department were also there. Andrea Conte, Verna Wyatt, and Valerie Craig from *You Have the Power* are always there. We, who have been affected by violent crime, appreciate all those who continue to be involved in crime victim's ceremonies and the continued effort to reduce violent crime.

In addition to the dignitaries that night, were about 250-300 friends and family members of murder victims. It was cold and many were sitting under a huge tent. Others stood around the outer edges of the tent, huddled closely together—maybe to hear what was being said, or perhaps trying to stay a little warmer from the propane heaters in the corners of the tent. I knew a lot of the people, but many of the faces were new to me.

The ceremony had grown over the years. The location had changed from the Mayor's office in the courthouse to Centennial Park a few years earlier. Mayor Purcell had a tree planted that would become the ceremonial Christmas tree. Ornaments with faces of departed loved ones; sayings and poems in glitter sparkled from the tree's white lights. From the second Thursday in December until January 2, these ornaments hang in memory of our loved ones.

I am thankful, not just for the dignitaries and other officials, but for the friends and families of the victims. These people are why the ceremony exists. It is an emotional ceremony, especially for the new people. We draw strength from those who understand this time of year can be extremely difficult to get through.

Waves of emotions hit; depression, loneliness, anger, and other negative feelings, but, for an hour we find comfort in the company of others who have been thrown into a grief like ours. We think this joyous time of year can no longer be joyous. In fact until we reach what Dr. Elisabeth Kübler-Ross defines as the fifth stage of grief: *Acceptance*, we think we can't find joy in the season.

Therapy: It Does a Mind Good

The Victim Intervention Program is a counseling service through the Metropolitan Nashville Police Department. The department offers free counseling to victims of violent crimes and to their family members. The counselors have at least a master's degree and they are kind and gentle souls who listen well. When I called asking for help, the director of VIP, Amy Griffith said, my one on one counselor would be Heidi Bennett. It had been fifty-one weeks since Carl had been murdered. As the one-year anniversary approached I realized I had focused more time on taking care of my parents, Mom after Dad died, and I had not yet taken care of myself.

My mother went to VIP a couple of weeks after Carl's funeral and it helped her. My father on the other hand would not go, would not talk about Carl, the murder, the investigation or anything else having to do anything with life. I spent an hour a week, for ten or twelve weeks with Heidi. She was such a gift, an angel sent from heaven.

After a few months of one-on-one counseling, the program offers group counseling. We have given it the name "The Forever Group." Many people who are thrown into a world of violence and lose a loved one are forever bonded with others who find themselves in the same place.

They Are Not Forgotten

Martha Wyatt

One of the first people I met when I started group counseling at VIP in 1995 was Verna Wyatt. Verna's sister-in-law and best friend Martha Wyatt was murdered in 1991. Martha was forty-two years old, a wife and mother, and a homebound schoolteacher. One day when she arrived at the home of her student, the student's mother's boyfriend met her at the front door. No one else was home. He raped Martha, beat her and wrapped her in a tarp and threw her body in the Cumberland River. The autopsy revealed Martha drown, she wasn't dead when her body was "thrown away." Verna has been a great mentor to me. Since Martha's death, Verna lives her life with passion and purpose; helping victims of crime reclaim their lives.

Sarah Jackson

Jerry and Gina Jackson's sixteen-year-old daughter Sarah was murdered on the morning of February 16, 1997. Jerry, Gina, and Sarah's brother Wayne all have a special place in my heart. This sweet family was forever changed when Sarah was murdered at the Captain D's restaurant in Donelson, Tennessee.

A man entered under the guise of applying for a job. Paul Dennis Reid, a serial killer, forced Sarah, and her twenty-five-year-old manager, Steve Hampton into the cooler. He forced them to lie on the floor and then shot them in the head execution-style. He robbed them and the restaurant. Reid's fingerprint was found on a movie card in Hampton's wallet, which he had tossed along the roadside. Two days after the murders, Reid used some of the money from the robbery to prepay the lease on a car. (Sarah was one of eight victims assaulted by Reid in three robberies at fast food establishments.) Reid was later convicted on seven counts of first-degree murder across three trials. Jose Antonio Rameriz Gonzalez, the lone surviving victim of a McDonald's robbery, identified Reid in court as his attacker.

Marcia Trimble

Virginia Trimble is the mother of Marcia Trimble who I mentioned in Chapter one. Virginia endured thirty plus years not knowing who killed her little girl. This is one of the oldest cold cases to be recently solved in Nashville. Through DNA and great police work, Marcia's killer was brought to justice on July 18, 2009. A jury convicted 62-year-old Jerome Barrett of two counts of second-degree murder. Barrett was sentenced to 44 years in prison.

Jason White

My heart smiled when I asked Anna White for her permission to share her son, Jason's story. Anna said, "Yes, you have my permission and I am thankful that someone still wants to remember Jason in some way."

On August 5, 1996, Jason and his girlfriend stopped at a convenience store to buy a soda. He had worked hard for the Saturn car with nice rims. Three guys (two were on parole at the time) followed Jason as he exited the interstate. The thugs carjacked him, shot him twice, once in the leg and once in the chest. When Jason's car was found there was one fingerprint that led the police to the killers. Three men were tried, convicted, and sentenced to prison. The shooter received life, plus twenty years. The second received seventy-five years, the driver that let his buddies out at the market, received a prison sentence of fifteen years. Jason White was eighteen years old.

Jamie Marable

Jim Marable's daughter, Jamie, was 19 years old when her murdered body was found on September 12, 1990. She had been stabbed to death with a screwdriver some days earlier.

Her father has been heart-broken ever since. Jim and his family had to wait six years before the murderer was charged and sent to prison with a life sentence. The life sentence was later overturned on appeal and reduced to second-degree murder.

Jim is a great guy. He was a real friend to my mother after the two of them wound up in the same counseling group. *Thanks Jim for being so kind to Mom. She has a special bond with you and will love you forever, as will I.*

Craig Spain

Sherry Spain's brother, Craig Spain, was a gifted, 42-year-old artist. He created set designs for local performing arts theaters. He was a wonderful brother to Sherry and a very loving son to his parents Ken and Virginia. Craig was murdered on May 14, 1996. Sherry found her brother's body in the hall of his home. He had been stabbed multiple times.

Melissa Chilton & Tiffany Campbell

Gail Chilton's daughter, Melissa was 18 years old when she and co-worker, Tiffany Campbell were stabbed to death by an unknown assailant while at work in 1996. For many years Gail, Virginia Trimble and I shared the only cold cases in the Forever Group. In July 2009, Gail and I spent a week sitting in a courtroom with Virginia while the man who murdered her daughter Marcia, was tried and convicted. I hope one day Virginia and I can sit in the courtroom for Gail, while the killer of her daughter is tried.

Justin Green

Mary Jane Green's son, Justin played football for his high school. He never got a chance to graduate; he was 15 years old when he was murdered in 2003. He and his brother were home playing video games when two intruders entered the home in a botched robbery attempt—leaving Justin lying face down in his bedroom with a fatal gunshot wound to his chest.

Keith Crabtree Dawson

Steve Dawson and Brenda Crabtree's son Keith Crabtree Dawson was murdered when he was 18 years old. Keith was shot to death on September 17, 2000. He died after being shot twice with a .22 long rifle at a friend's apartment. For several years before her death in 2007, Brenda was a staunch advocate for crime victim's rights. She died of cancer in March 2007. While planning her own funeral, she asked, "In lieu of flowers, I would like you to laugh, not take things too seriously, and say, 'I love you' to the people in your life because life is too short. Give them a hug and tell them a joke as well."

Wayne Hedge

One other member of the Forever Group is Sheila. Yes, my Sheila. Her brother-in-law Wayne Hedge was murdered in July 1985. Wayne gave a friend a ride home from a softball game and got caught in a domestic violence situation that left him and the girl he took home dead from shotgun wounds. The killer was apprehended and charged, tried and convicted with two first-degree murder charges.

When I first met Sheila she hadn't talked to anyone but her medical doctor about her grief. The doctor gave her a prescription and advised her to exercise to help work through her grief. I asked her to tell me about Wayne. I wanted her to open up and share with me what she was feeling. She did and she felt better the more we talked. I spent a week in August of '86 in a Davidson County courtroom with Sheila and her family. Who would have ever imagined she would become my support only eight years later when my brother Carl was murdered?

After I went to counseling at VIP and became a part of the Forever Group, I encouraged Sheila to go to one on one counseling at VIP. "Work with people who know what they are doing," I said. It had been about eleven years since Wayne was murdered when Sheila found counselors who helped her move through her own pain. It is a rare thing to have a loved one murdered and we share that truth in both our families.

Verna, Jerry and Gina, Virginia, Anna, Jim, Sherry, Gail, Mary Jane, Steve, Brenda and Sheila, you are all in my heart. Thank you for supporting me in some of the most difficult days of my life. My hope is I have done the same for you.

There are so many others I have not named who at some time or other participated in The Forever Group. I wish I could name each one and their loved one and what happened to each of them. Michael Bouchette was only 20 and attending Cumberland University when he was murdered. Blue Robinson was 24, Tandy Fletcher was 71, Dean Finchum was 58, Whitney Boone was killed when she was 16 years old. Jo Jo Hempel was 21, Dominic Houston was 17, Lynn Hicks was 35, Willie Houston was 38, William Jackson was 29, Nathan Long was 66, Brook McCormick was 22 when she was murdered. Darrell McKisskick, Jr. was 24, Pamela Orend was 47 when she was abducted, raped, murdered, and thrown in a ditch. This woman had a husband named Jack who loved her dearly. Each one of these murder victims has people who love and miss them. Timothy Pigg was 31, Torey Pillow was 19, Bill Reynolds was 41. Shirley Rich's son, Bert Rich was 29.

Shirley, like Jim was part of my Mother's group. My mother has a bond with her because of the beginning days of counseling. Troy Snell was 18 when he was murdered. I got to know his sweet mother Billie from attending The Forever Group. Jason Wilkerson was 20; he was murdered by a man who wanted to know what it felt like to shoot someone.

All of these names represent a family that has had to endure the loss of a loved one due to the senseless act of another. Many of these murder victims I feel like I know personally, but how could I? I met their loved one after the fact. I listed these sweet souls' names because after a person dies their name is not often seen in print, and I want to honor their memory by recognizing the fact they were once here. They are not forgotten.

Many of these names get a face each year at *A Season to Remember*. After the formalities of the ceremony, families and friends line up in a single file. We wait to approach the microphone where our loved ones name is spoken, sending the sound wave out into the universe, I say *"My brother Carl Williams."* We then walk a few feet to the tree and place a homemade ornament to hang throughout the holiday season.

I was honored when asked to give the speech at the 2009 ceremony. When asked, I had been writing this book for about two months, and what I was learning from the process was changing my life. As I began to prepare for my speech I knew I could not stand in front of hundreds of people and tell a sad story of Carl being murdered. I wanted to share a message of hope and peace and joy. The following is an excerpt from my speech in 2009:

A Season to Remember

I know there are many of you here who are hurting. I remember that pain. Grief that is so heavy inside it almost squeezes the very breath from your being. The blanket of fog that blurs your mind; I remember that fog too. Homicide may be what has brought us together; there is a bond among people who have lost a loved one to murder. Often times you don't feel comfortable talking to people about your loved one and the pain you feel. I know there is nothing I can say to make you feel better. I wish I could wave a magic wand and take all of your pain away, but I can't. What I can do is tell you I love you and I am here if you ever need someone to talk to, or need someone to listen.

We all require time to grieve. In the Bible, in Matthew 5:4, Jesus says, "Blessed are they that mourn: for they shall be comforted."

After many, many years of suffering, the peace inside of me only came when I chose to remember Carl in a positive light instead of allowing my mind to focus on the murder or murderer. What happened to him was far beyond my control. I could do nothing to help with the investigation, but I felt like I needed to do something. If you haven't heard of or seen the quote by Mahatma Gandhi on something from VIP or You Have the Power, you haven't been around here very long. I love this quote; it speaks to me. Gandhi said, "You must be the change you wish to see in the world."

I have changed and I want to help people understand that we don't have to continue to suffer year after year. I want to encourage you to live your lives on purpose and not feel like your life has been destroyed. Your loved one's life was taken by force but don't willingly give up on yours. You may be down right now and that is understandable. It took me a long time to realize all I had control over was how I reacted to this. I now know the thoughts I hold in my mind determine how I react or respond to things. Realizing I have a choice was when the shift happened for me. Peace came to me when I began to THiNK peace.

The Thinking Rock Story

As Sheila and I walked along the beach in South Beach, Miami, I noticed the sand being a little rockier than I had expected. In comparison to a speck of sand, there were large rocks. I spotted one that grabbed my attention. After I bent down and washed it off, the rock looked like the Nike logo. You know, the SWOOSH? The rock was smooth and rounded and about an inch long. Carrying this rock in my pocket made me smile, I thought of Nike's slogan, "Just Do It." Carrying this rock with me made me feel like I could do anything. I transformed "Just Do It" into "I can do it."

I carried this rock with me every day—for several years. This rock was my very first THINKING ROCK. As I continued writing the book, or toying with the idea of writing a book and carrying my rock, my thoughts began to change.

I was reading more books than I have ever read in my life and I was learning how powerful our minds are. All because I thought I could write a book and tell people how to overcome life's challenges. I guess God knew I wanted to be of service. But before I could help others, I had to help myself. That is what the Nike rock did for me. From the time I found the "I can do it" rock on South Beach, to when I really *believed* I could do it, four years had passed. When I started paying attention to my thoughts, I noticed my moods were in line with my thinking. When I thought "bad" or "negative" things, I felt bad and acted negatively. Knowing my life cannot be filled with joy and happiness if I am feeling and thinking negative things, I began to shift my thinking.

As I progressed through this newfound, optimistic way of looking at life, my mind started opening. This was good for me, but bad for most everyone around me. I thought out loud too often. People got sick of hearing me talk about thinking. I know now what was happening, I was unlearning things I had been taught. *If I change my thinking, can I change my life?* This is the question I asked. People got sick of it. I eventually learned I could not tell anyone what to do, think, or believe.

When I turned my questioning inward my personal growth began.

Seeds of Peace

Oprah Winfrey is the first person I ever heard say, "When you know better, you do better." I recently learned Oprah learned this wonderful lesson from her friend and mentor, Maya Angelou. I have a tendency to be very matter of fact; a straightforward kind of person, too serious for my own good sometimes. Knowing I was going to be giving the speech at *A Season to Remember*, I tried to write my message in a way that says, "When you know better, you do better."

I also wanted people to know that they can do it.

We can think of our loved ones and not get depressed, or mad and angry because they were murdered. But how could I say that and it not sound inconsiderate or insensitive? I wanted everyone there who had lost a loved one to know peace. I wanted them to know joy and happiness again in their lives. How could I share this message of hope and peace with people, knowing they were feeling like their hearts were being ripped out from the grief? I couldn't help but think of Charles Haanel's quote.

> *"Hidden in the method of our thoughts lies the power to create our ideal world."*

That is when I knew what I had to share—if we want peace, we have to think peace. We cannot think horrible thoughts or wish something had never happened, and ever have a sense of peace.

Knowing we all go through grief at our own pace. We process through the stages of grief just as Kübler-Ross wrote about. We cannot tell anyone how to grieve, or when to grieve. It is an individual choice. We each get to decide how long we continue to replay the emotion, running it through the loop again and again. When we are ready, we will move forward.

With each thought of our loved one, as we begin to reflect on the good and not the bad, slowly we move out of the pain and sadness.

For me this happened when I decided to shift my thoughts. Each time I thought about Carl, whether the thought was about his murder or the unsolved case, or that he wouldn't be here for the holidays, I changed my thought. I would no longer allow myself to think of things that happened as if I could somehow change them. I would not let myself stay in a place of wishing things were different.

As I began to make this thought flow a habit, my joy, and happiness returned. I was able to think of Carl and feel gratitude for having known him, versus feeling sad and depressed because things were not the way I would have liked them to be. The more I practiced this, the easier it got. Death is not the opposite of life, birth is. We are born and then we die and somewhere in between there is life. Instead of focusing on the death, I now choose to focus on his life and his continuing spirit.

Thankfully when I think of my brother, the murder is no longer the first thing that pops into my mind. A smile usually comes across my face when I think of him. Memories flood my mind, which eventually turn into a feeling of light and love like I have never known. Instead of feeling sad, I feel a warm embrace, like he is hugging me saying he is fine and telling me I am doing pretty well too.

Just as a farmer plants seeds for what he chooses to grow, I planted seeds of peace within my mind. For the ceremony, I ordered little silver plastic peace signs from a novelty company and paid my great niece's Ciara and Brianna and my great nephew Chas to sew the peace sign on a business card that read: Seeds of Peace. I gave each person a card as they approached the microphone to say their loved ones name, just before hanging their ornament on the tree.

God told me once, *Quit telling people what to do.* So instead of telling people to think peace, I shared, "To have peace, you first have to think peace." I also printed on the card, "If you ever need someone to just listen, call me, Connie Williams, and my cell number."

What most of us in the West are not taught; is a quiet mind cureth all. I believe silence is the language of God and for me to hear God I have to be quiet. After a loved one is murdered, or when anything happens in our life that is tragic, for some reason we play it over and over again in our minds. Like a movie projector, we keep hitting replay.

Having peace in our lives is only possible when we are able to understand that bad things happen. Peace is not the absence of conflict, but the ability to cope with it in a way that it doesn't rob us of our happiness. Not everything is going to go according to our plan, life doesn't happen exactly like we want it to. When we can deal with what comes our way with an understanding and the knowledge that we have the power within to endure all things, we can live every day with inner peace.

Chapter 9

The Impetus That Moves Us Forward
Love is unconditional and eternal

> *"I have found the paradox, that if you love until it hurts, there can be no more hurt, only more love."*
>
> ~ Mother Teresa
> (1910-1997) Roman Catholic Nun,
> Noble Peace Prize winner

Neighbor Jay

As my neighbor Jay lay dying in the winter of 2009-2010, sometimes I sat with him. At that time this book was a work in progress and a couple of times he asked me, "How is the book coming?" Which lead to an interesting conversation a few days before he passed. Trying to control the pain from cancer that had eaten into his bones, he was drugged from the morphine patch that was stuck to his body. As we talked for a little while, at one point I told Jay that unless something unexpected happened to me, it looked like his journey on earth was going to end before mine.

I asked him if he had any words of wisdom to share with a novice writer. Because of the divine message I received earlier that year, *you need to quit telling people what to do;* I shared with Jay that I was trying my best to not tell people what to do. I asked him to share some words of wisdom. Jay looked at me, a glazed look in his eyes, but with total lucidity, said these words....

"Just ask them.... how much heart do you give away?"

Wow, I thought, and then said, *Jay that is beautiful, thank you.* This came from a very rough and tough Texan who had never shown this kind of sensitivity. Facing the end of our journey in this life must make us think and say things that we normally wouldn't say. Jay was kind, he was a great man, and he was very expressive, but not in a soft heartfelt way.

Some of my fondest memories of Jay are when we'd sit out on his deck, drink a beer, and talk about everything from the music business in Nashville to God in heaven or Buddha.

He was always interested in mine and Sheila's real estate business and what current project we had going. He'd yell across the street to me, and say, "Come over, let's us girls just talk." He was a man with a great sense of humor. We were honored when Bettye, his bride (that is what Jay often called Bettye), asked us to speak at Jay's memorial service. We love our neighbors and I am grateful I got to have that last conversation with Jay.

Too many times for me to count I have asked myself—how much heart do I give away? Especially in times my feathers get ruffled. Jay left us with a powerful question.

The Aim of Living

When I first started writing this book it was because I wanted to help people understand that grieving doesn't have to last forever. It is okay to smile when we think of our loved ones who have passed on.

The two-and-one-half year writing process has changed me. I have become a new person. I know the hurt that Mother Teresa spoke of. "I never stopped going through the hurt until I came out on the other side with only love." The process is not fun, and requires patience, but in the end, it's worth it. We all have a purpose in life. If you haven't discovered why you are here, please allow me to inform you. You are here because you are unique and special. The world needs you just the way you are. You matter, and I challenge you to unpack the thoughts you have and see what they tell you about you and your life.

As we begin to understand our thinking, we begin to understand our purpose. I think Jay knew the purpose of life is to love one another. It sounds like a simple reason for us to be on this planet. The whole reason for loving unconditionally, finding our passions, and living with purpose; if packed up in the smallest one word explanation is—LOVE.

Love is the impetus that moves all things. We as humans find it difficult to wrap our brains around unconditional love. Sure we know what it means. I had unconditional love from my parents. It was given to me and I learned what love is. Nonetheless, at some point in my life I chose to begin setting conditions on love. I am not sure when that happened but through judgment, inexperience, naivety, and stupidity, I turned love into "sometimes love."

When I began to see people as different from me, I severed the oneness. If and when I allow my thoughts, beliefs, and actions to anything but love, I have changed unconditional love to conditional love. Love with conditions is not love at all.

> *Every struggle of the mind—be it struggle against pain, struggle against appetite, struggle for more skill in the doing of anything, struggle for greater advance in any art or calling, struggle and dissatisfaction at your failings and defects – is an actual pushing of the spirit to greater power, and a greater relative completion of yourself – and with such completion, happiness. For the aim of living is happiness."*

~Prentice Mulford, *Thoughts Are Things*

Notice Prentice Mulford did not take aim at being happy. Instead he said, the aim of living, *is* happiness.

Think back to a time when you were completely happy. I don't mean happy for a day or a week, I mean happy with every part of your life and you felt good every day, no matter what happened. I have always thought of myself as having a really good life. For the most part I was happy, but then again not really. As far back as I can remember I would think, "if only this or if only that, then I'd be happy. If only my parents had more money, they wouldn't have to struggle financially."

I was a tomboy growing up, so I often thought *if only I could be as cute and feminine as everyone wants me to be, that might make me happy.* As I entered high school, I was athletic, with a muscular build, people called me "stocky." Imagine what that does to a 15-year old girl's self-esteem. We begin to believe the conditioning of our culture, the lessons from our teachers, the beliefs of our families, and the actions of our neighbors.

We got by, we had food, shelter and clothing, but I didn't think that way back then. Imagine if I had been grateful for what we had instead of worrying about whether the electricity was going to get turned off. Even after Sheila and I got together, I was happy. But was I really? I think not, because I was not aiming to live. I was aiming to be happy, find happiness, make more money, change my body, find a better job, or start another business. I was happy being with Sheila; but thinking all these other things could bring me happiness was not real.

The search for happiness in outer things is endless, it cannot be found on the outside. We are hard on ourselves as we go through life. Once we get out of the minutia and understand that there are far greater things to focus on is when real change can come about. When we are too caught up in the details and worry, our mind is distracted. We are as far from being conscious. When we begin to harness the power of universal laws and have the awareness to use them in our lives, we can redirect our course.

As we begin to understand that thoughts are things and these things are what make our life what it is, we can change our lives. The inquiry, the self-discovery and acceptance of reality are what move us forward. We first have to love ourselves enough to begin the process of understanding the aim of living is happiness. We have to live on purpose. We can only do this with the help of the universe and the laws and principles that govern this planet we live on.

Introduction to Universal Laws and Principles

There are universal laws in force in all of our lives. Whether you believe in the forces makes no difference, they are still working in your life. No matter what we try to do we're all born and we will all die. What we need to know is we must abide by certain laws in order to create the life we want to live.

There are universal laws and principles that control everything in life.

These laws are not debatable. We don't have to believe in Newton's Law of Universal Gravitation (gravity), for it to be present in our life. Just as the universal law of gravity is at work in our lives so are other universal laws.

Our thoughts are powerful and our ability to choose what thoughts to hold in our mind is what makes a successful life. Simply stated if you want to change your life, change the way you think. This is the Law of Attraction. Unconditional love, the law of attraction, and all things metaphysical are part of us.

For centuries scientists have tried to explain God, the universe and all its power. Whether you are an individual who needs explanations or someone who lives by faith alone, I encourage you to ask yourself, "Why are things the way they are?" By things, I mean your life, work, your relationships, community, country, and the world. I challenge you to set all judgment aside and look inwardly. Your answers might surprise you— mine did. In fact, as the answers evolved so did I, thankfully, and so did this book.

Writing *THiNKING CONSCIOUSLY ROCKS* has been an arduous process for me. I have grown so much as an individual and I wouldn't trade this experience for anything.

Newton's Law of Universal Gravitation

Newton saw God as the master creator whose existence could not be denied in the face of the grandeur of all creation. He said, "These principles were available for all people to discover, allowed people to pursue their own aims fruitfully in this life, and to perfect themselves with their own rational powers." We don't have to understand the mechanics of Newton's Law of Universal Gravitation to benefit from its powers. We don't have to know point mass (m_1) attracts another point mass (m_2) by a force (F2) which is proportional to the product of the two masses and inversely proportional to the square of the distance (r) between them. Regardless of masses or distance, the magnitudes of (F_1) and (F_2) will always be equal. G is the gravitational constant.

In a world where change is inevitable, I find it comforting knowing there are a few things that are constant.

Newton's Laws of Motion

You may not know Sir Isaac Newton's 3rd Law of Motion; but I am pretty sure you have heard of its existence: The Law of Reciprocal Actions. "To every action there is always an equal and opposite reaction..." Much easier explained, there is no such thing as something for nothing.

This law actually says an object will always continue moving at its current speed and in its current direction until some force causes its speed or direction to change. This would include an object that is not in motion (velocity = zero), which will remain at rest until some force causes it to move.

We are often the objects that are not in motion, velocity equals zero. In other words we are going nowhere. Or perhaps we are in motion, but we continue to live the same day over and over again, we have no heading, no direction and we are not happy with our lives.

As much as I respect Newton and his wisdom, I choose to translate this wonderful discovery of the law of reciprocal actions into something which I can understand— for change to occur something has to change. Our lives as we know them are a direct result of the mental attitude that we have towards life. Period. It is known as karma in the East, or in the Bible, as reaping what you've sewn—what goes around comes around.

We know this stuff, we have heard it all our lives but we have never understood our role.

There are so many times in life now that I draw on the Old Lady/Young Lady paradigm. Understanding we don't all see things the same way and knowing that our brains process incoming data in different ways helps me respect the beliefs of others. In other words, I am using the Law of Cause and Effect to receive and give that which I want in life. If I do not allow the other person to see the old lady when I see the young lady I am never going to have love, peace, and harmony in my life?

When I allow people to have their own opinions and I don't try to change them or make them see it my way, I get to live a life of peace.

This state of being is what I believe the Bible calls "the peace that passes all understanding." We cannot physically or mentally comprehend the magnitude of this power. This is the same power Eckhart Tolle refers to in his book *The Power of Now*. Tolle teaches the way to live truly is to live consciously and in the now. I think living with an open heart and being united with all that is, versus being closed-hearted and divided from the whole is what makes us happy or sad.

If this information is totally new to you, bear with me, we have a long way to go. There is a lot more information that I know will leave you with a sense of wonder and if I have done my job when you finish this book you will have more questions than answers. The truth is, as we learn more about ourselves and others, and about our planet; we begin to sense the fullness of life.

My objective is to promote conscious thinking. Thinking for ourselves, asking questions of ourselves that we normally wouldn't take the time to ask. Socrates said, "We learn best through self-discovery." What I have discovered is; we as a culture seldom take the time to slow down long enough to have any deep thoughts—philosophical or otherwise. Self-discovery can only happen when we dive deeply into ourselves and look at how and what we think about, instead of diving in and out of our drama or other people's problems.

Kings and queens alike have said, "It is far easier to rule a kingdom than to rule one's own mind." It takes being the ruler of our own mind to create the life we want to live. We can either choose to create our life by controlling our mind; what we think about and the information we allow to come into our minds, or we can continue being controlled by life and its circumstances.

As we begin to think about things in new ways, we begin to discover, uncover, appreciate, and love life as it is. This is the place where real change can happen. This is the place where we choose to live in the moment, give up having to be right, or wanting things to be different than they are.

The Law of Cause and Effect

Our life is what we make it; the evolving of our spirit is in direct correlation with the law of cause and effect. Sometimes things happen in our life and we ask, "What in the world did I do to cause this?" Let me share a secret: when asking what caused *that* something—we are actually asking—what is the cause of this effect? The effect is the result of the cause, not the other way around.

The cause starts in our mind and the effect shows up in our life. Like Newton's third law—for every action there is an equal and opposite reaction. When we take action and tell someone what to do, why are we surprised when other people tell us what to do? If we don't want people telling us what to do, we have to stop telling others what to do. If we want to know unconditional love, we must first give unconditional love. If our life is in turmoil and we are seeking peace, we must first be peaceful to allow peace to grow within us. We cannot have peace if we do not think peace. We get what we think.

If we think we need more, don't have enough money, hate our job, or are sick all of the time, how can we expect anything positive to come from those negative thoughts? We must think love, gratitude, peace, and vision. To know unconditional love, we must give love. Have you ever heard the song by Cheryl Crow, *Soak up the Sun*? I love the lyric in the first verse that says, "*It's not having what you want, it's wanting what you've got.*"

To be blessed with more, we first must be grateful for what we have. Before I could ever have inner peace about my brother Carl being murdered, I had to think peace. I could not be peaceful while thinking thoughts of him getting shot in the head, his head lying in a pool of blood, or the officials discovering his body lying on the shoulder of the interstate. As I began to think of him in a different way, when my thoughts changed to the memories we shared, then peace came to me.

We cannot love what we do each day when we hate our jobs. We cannot love our work until we are doing something we love doing. Before we can find something we love doing, we first have to have vision. What does that dream job look like? If time and money were not a problem, what would you do? Who would you be? As you begin to visualize what that life looks like, you'll notice your current life will improve as well. Being kind and loving at work, being grateful for the job you currently have and thinking about the work you would love to do, will draw your dream job to you. This stuff works. You might be a skeptic and that is okay. It took me years to grasp and understand the little I do.

I know there is so much that I do not know about the laws and principles of the universe. If I thought I knew, I would be putting God in a box. I know God is bigger than any problem I have. I cannot fully understand the magnitude of God because I am human, but I know my spirit soars when I make the connection.

The connection is made when I think consciously and live my life on purpose. The connection is made when I am present and sit quietly in the presence of spirit. The connection is made when I am kind and loving. When I am in this place my aim is right on target, love moves me forward and I am filled with happiness. My cup runneth over. Living in this place, life is easier to manage. The majority of times things don't get to me. I say the majority, because I am human after all and sometimes I can be a jerk—but the more I live here instead of there, the easier life is.

iPods, iTunes & iTalk

In 2010 Sheila and I started a podcast. Three weeks before our first episode was on iTunes we didn't know what a podcast was. We had a message and we wanted to share that message. We talked to Jonathan Nation about developing a website and he told us what we wanted and needed was a podcast. We are forever grateful to him for introducing us to Podcamp Nashville. Less than two weeks after we talked to Jonathan we met Cliff Ravenscraft (www.PodcastAnswerman.com) at Podcamp Nashville. One week after we met Cliff, he spent a day with us setting up our equipment, getting www.ConnieandSheilaTalk.com online, and getting our podcast on iTunes.

It was amazing how quickly these two men took our desire to share our message and guided us into our online radio show that is now heard in 66 countries and all 50 U.S. States. After finding our own show on iTunes, I played around on iTunes looking at the thousands and thousands of talk show titles. There is a show for everything. If you want to hear two women talk about *Real Life, Real Estate, Real Fun* stuff; listen to us on *Connie and Sheila Talk*. If you want to learn how to quilt, cook, hunt, build race cars, manage your finances, meditate, get the latest news, speak another language, hear great stories from wonderful storytellers or just listen to someone talk about the latest hot new television series, you can find a podcast because podcasters talk about everything.

Some of the podcasts I have subscribe to are: *Eckhart Tolle TV*, *Oprah.com's Spirit Channel*, *The Smart Passive Income*, *Podcast Answerman*, *Joel Osteen Video Podcast*, *Marianne Williamson's Miracle Thought*, *48 Days LLC with Dan Miller*, *This American Life*, *Tara Brach*, *MorningCoach.com*, and a whole host of others. On average, I follow about thirty shows in my iTunes library. I learn a lot from listening to the advice and experience of others.

One of the most interesting stories I ever heard on a podcast was from a monk of the Thai Forest tradition who lives in a monastery near Perth, Australia. Ajahn Brahm was born Peter Betts in London on August 7, 1951. He came from a working class background and won a scholarship to study Theoretical Physics at Cambridge University in the late 1960s. After graduating from Cambridge he taught high school for one year before traveling to Thailand to become a monk and train with the Venerable Ajahn Chah.

He is the author of two books, *Mindfulness, Bliss & Beyond* (2006) and *Opening the Door of Your Heart* (2005). *Opening the Door of Your Heart* was first published under the title *Who Ordered This Truckload of Dung?* While listening to one of his podcast episodes I heard Ajahn Brahm tell this story: (Thank you Ajahn Brahm for permission to share your story.)

A Truckload of Dung

Unpleasant things, like coming in last in our class, happen in life. They happen to everyone. The only difference between a happy person and one who gets depressed is how they respond to disasters.

Imagine you have just had a wonderful afternoon at the beach with a friend. When you return home, you find a huge truckload of dung has been dumped right in front of your door. There are three things to know about this truckload of dung:

- You did not order it. It's not your fault.

- You're stuck with it. No one saw who dumped it, so you cannot call anyone to take it away.

- It is filthy and offensive, and its stench fills your whole house. It is almost impossible to endure.

    In this metaphor, the truckload of dung in front of the house stands for the traumatic experiences that are dumped on us in life. As with the truckload of dung, there are three things to know about tragedy in our life:

1. We did not order it. It's not our fault. We say, "Why me?"

2. We're stuck with it. No one, not even the ones who love us most dearly, can take it away (though they may try).

3. It is so awful, such a destroyer of our happiness and its pain fills our whole life. It is almost impossible to endure.

    There are two ways of responding to being stuck with the truckload of dung. The first way is to carry the dung around with us. We put some in our pockets, some in our backpacks and briefcases, and some up our shirts. We even put some down our pants. We find when we carry dung around; we lose a lot of friends! Even best friends don't seem to be around so often.

"Carrying around the dung" is a metaphor for sinking into depression, negativity, or anger. It is a natural and understandable response to adversity. But we lose a lot of friends, because it is also natural and understandable that our friends don't like being around us when we're so depressed. Moreover, the pile of dung doesn't get any smaller and, what's more, the smell gets worse as it ripens.

Fortunately, there's a second way. When a truckload of dung is dumped in front of our house, we heave a sigh and then get down to work. Out come the wheelbarrow, the fork, and the spade. We fork the dung into the barrow, wheel it around the back of the house, and dig it into the garden. This is tiring and difficult work, but we know there's no other useful option.

Sometimes, all we can manage is a half a barrow a day. But even so, we're doing something about the problem, rather than complaining our way into depression. Day after day we dig in the dung. Day after day, the pile gets a little smaller. Sometimes it takes several years, but the morning does come when we see that the dung in front of our house is all gone. Furthermore, a miracle has happened in another part of our house. The flowers in the garden are bursting out in richness of color all over the place. Their fragrance wafts down the street so that the neighbors, and even passers-by, smile in delight. Then the fruit tree in the corner is nearly falling over, it's so heavy with fruit. And the fruit is so sweet; you can't buy anything like it. There's so much of it that we are able to share it with our neighbors. Even passers-by get a delicious taste of the miracle fruit.

"Digging in the dung" is a metaphor welcoming the tragedies as fertilizer for life. It is work that we have to do alone: no one can help us here. But by digging it into the garden of our heart, day by day, the pile of pain gets less.

It may take us several years, but the morning does come when we see no more pain in our life and in, our heart, a miracle has happened. Flowers of kindness are bursting out all over the place, and the fragrance of love wafts way down our street, to our neighbors, to our relations, and even to passers-by. Then our wisdom tree in the corner is bending down to us, loaded with sweet insights into the nature of life. We share those delicious fruits freely, even with passers-by, without ever planning to.

When we have known pain, learned its lesson, and grown our garden, then we can put our arms around another in deep tragedy and say softly, "I know." They realize we do understand. Compassion begins. We show them the wheelbarrow, the fork and the spade, and boundless encouragement. Yet, if we haven't grown our own garden yet, it can't be done.

I have known many monks who are skilled in meditation, who are peaceful, composed, and serene in adversity. But only a few have become great teachers. I often wondered why.

It seems to me now that monks who had a relatively easy time of it, who had little dung to dig in, were the ones who didn't become great teachers. It was the monks who had the enormous difficulties, dug them in quietly, and came through with a rich garden that became great teachers. They all had wisdom, serenity, and compassion; but those with more dung had more to share with the world. My own teacher, Ajahn Chah, who for me was the pinnacle of all teachers, must have had a whole trucking company with a fleet of trucks delivering dung as his door in his early life.

Perhaps the moral of this story is that if you want to be of service to the world, if you wish to follow the path of compassion, then the next time a tragedy occurs in your life, you may say, "Whoopee! More fertilizer for my garden!

Opening the Door of Your Heart: And Other Buddhist Tales of Happiness

Ajahn Brahm, author Hachette Australia 2010
Reprinted with permission

Chapter 10

Conscious Awareness of All Things
A grateful heart

> *"Rejoice always, pray continually, give thanks in all circumstances; for this is God's will for you in Christ Jesus."*
>
> ~ 1 Thessalonians 5:16-18 (NIV)

When I was a kid I often wondered and even asked, *how do we pray continually?* I had grown up hearing the phrase "pray without ceasing," how is that physically possible? The way I had always prayed was on my knees at bedtime, before a meal, in times of need, to help a friend or while at church. When I prayed I talked to God. I asked God for things and sometimes I thanked God for things. No matter what the prayer or where I prayed, I talked. I talked and seldom listened. Being silent never occurred to me. For a long time I believed the scripture in Isaiah 40:31 (KJV) "But they that wait upon the LORD shall renew their strength; they shall mount up with wings as eagles; they shall run, and not be weary; and they shall walk, and not faint" to mean wait, as in doing nothing but wait.

The origin of the word wait comes from waiter, as in to serve. What do waiters do? They wait on you, they serve you, they are there trying to please you, doing the "right" things, waiting to be of good service. How had I missed the true meaning of this scripture? When I "wait" on God today it looks more like this: I try my best to do what is right. I treat people the way I want to be treated. I am kind and considerate and grateful for all things in my life.

I believe the language of God is silence. It is with a silent mind and still body that I now hear God. Instead of me talking the way I used to in prayer, my method of praying has changed. I think of myself like an EV. Electric vehicles (EVs) are propelled by an electric motor powered by rechargeable battery packs. They can go as far as two-hundred miles before they need recharging. A full recharge can take from four to eight hours, but in just thirty minutes, a quick charge can take them to eighty percent capacity.

My morning routine doesn't take a huge amount of time, each day I allow myself fifteen to thirty minutes to sit and connect with the power we share. This is my time to rejuvenate. I have to plug in and get my charge for the day. This power is what renews my strength so I shall mount up with wings as eagles, so I can run and not be weary, and walk and not faint. When I plug in each day, my battery gets charged. This energy makes me a better person and it makes my day more exciting and fulfilling. People are nicer to me, because I am nicer to them. My relationship with Sheila is more alive and tender. I am more aware. Life takes on a whole new meaning when I am being present. This is the place I can pray without ceasing, it is called Mindfulness.

Twinkling Presence and Midnight Skies

We stopped in La Esperanza to buy water for the thirteen of us, eight five-gallon bottles. Working with Heifer International Honduras, we were there to build shelter for a corn grinder that had been given to the people of Quebrada Honda. Dr. Trey was one of our thirteen member group, and he was to set up a make shift clinic.

The people of Quebrada Honda were happy to see the old blue school bus, maneuvering through ruts in the dirt road making its way to our new home. There is not a lot of traffic or people passing through this tiny Honduran city, they welcomed us by giving up the nicest house in the village—a tiny, blockhouse with concrete floors, no larger than 500 square feet. We were told a family of 14 stayed with others while we were in town. We were there for four days. I worked two of these days laying blocks, and two days fitting older Mayan descendants with reading glasses, and writing dosage instructions in Spanish on little plastic bags containing medicine, which Dr. Trey dispensed.

People walked for miles and some walked days to see the only doctor they'd seen in years, and for some, the only doctor they'd seen in their lifetime. It was a remarkable experience. The people, the place, the time and energy was palpable, like I have never known before. The people had so little, but wore a smile all day long. The topography of the land made it challenging for the children to play soccer, but they played anyway. Maybe it was just Sheila and I, thinking it was challenging. She played soccer with them several times and they never cared when the ball rolled down a huge hill. They'd just chase after it, run back up the hill, smiling the whole time, having tons of fun with Sheila.

It was as though time stood still there, and the advancing world had passed it by. There was no electricity or modern plumbing. We quit working before dark in time to get down the huge hill to our tiny village and our tiny house. None of the thirteen of us were ready or able to go to sleep when the sun went down, so we sat outside under the light of the moon and talked.

We didn't have a lot of water, so each night before going to bed Sheila and I would brush our teeth, rinsing with just a capful of water. I have never looked at clean, fresh water the same. At that time in my life, I had never heard of *being* present or being in the now. As I look back on that auspicious journey Now is where we were. The sky seemed larger and the stars closer and brighter. One night when Sheila and I made our way to the outhouse, we stood in awe. The sky looked like a painting. I can't help but think of two men, both born in the 1800s who said a thing or two about stars.

"If the stars should appear one night in a thousand years, how would men believe and adore, and preserve for many generations the remembrance of the city of God which had been shown!" ~ Emerson

Many of us are familiar with the painting *Starry Night*, painted by Vincent Van Gogh. This piece was painted during one of the most difficult periods of his life, while he was locked up in an asylum at Saint Remy. He painted the scene from memory. In letters to his brother Theo, Van Gogh mentioned *Starry Night* only twice. It is therefore one of the more mysterious and intriguing Van Gogh compositions.

Breathing Easy

Enjoying the stars and standing in awe of their creator, is being *conscious*. Conscious awareness allows me to rejoice always, pray continually, and give thanks in all circumstances. I later realized being in this place, not Honduras, but the now is what allows us to pray without ceasing.

You may ask, "How can I be thankful at all times, when this is not the life I want to live?

My neighbor Jay used to smoke four packs of cigarettes a day. That is about one every ten minutes; I think they call that chain smoking. Breathing is a natural part of living. We don't have to think about it, the brain and body work together, and it just happens.

One night I saw an ambulance in front of Jay's house. He was 64 and his wife Bettye was 78 at the time, I ran over to see if I could help. Just as I got to the front porch the EMT's were bringing Jay out on a stretcher. He was sitting up and his eyes were literally about to pop out of his head. He was gasping for breath like he had just spent five minutes under water. It was a scary sight. He could not breathe.

While at the hospital he was diagnosed with emphysema, Jay quit smoking that night. Five years later on his 69th birthday Jay was diagnosed with bone cancer and he died seven months after that, leaving his 83-year-old Bettye a widow.

If you think you have nothing to be thankful for, you are mistaken. You have 23,040 reasons every day. With each breath there is life. What comes so easy and natural for many of us, some people would die for. Easy breathing and a good deep breath is something to always be grateful for. Think about that the next time you feel like your life sucks or when you are having a pity party because you feel like life is passing you by.

Taking a few deep breaths can bring you back to the present moment—which is the only place where we can think gratitude!

My Brother Mike's a Saint

When I was a teenager, my oldest brother Mike worked at a residential facility for mentally and physically challenged adults and children. One time Mike took me to work with him. He wasn't going in to work, but had to stop by and pick something up. We weren't inside more than a minute before I was frightened by a noise. Inside the "big girls" unit was a constant ((((THUD)))), ((((THUD)))), ((((THUD)))). As I asked him what the sound was, he was already heading in the direction of the noise. It was at night and the girls were supposed to be in bed. He told me sometimes one of the girls gets up in the middle of the night and goes to the bathroom and sits on the floor. She repeatedly bangs her head against the block wall, over and over until someone rescues her from herself.

I followed my brother as he hurriedly made his way to this girl. As he sat down beside her, I was moved by his tenderness and care towards her. He rubbed her head with one hand, while wrapping his arm around her. Cradling and rocking her, he asked me to feel the knots that had formed on her skull; he then helped her up and led her back to bed. I have always wondered if that girl was trying to tell everyone, "Hey, I am in here. I may not be able to talk but I am here. Help me."

Thinking on Purpose

Thinking is another involuntary process of being human. Unless of course you have brain damage or a disorder that keeps your brain from working as it's designed to do. Studies have shown we have between 12,000 and 60,000 thoughts per day. Just like breathing, we don't have to think about thinking—we just do it. If we choose to, we can think about thinking.

When we think about breathing we can control our breaths, slow our heart rate, and relax. Which means our mind is powerful and autonomous. Having autonomy, we can govern our thoughts. They don't all have to happen automatically or subconsciously. By consciously guarding our thoughts, we can foster our dreams, goals, and passion. Life can be all that we want it to be.

Sometimes we allow life to make us unhappy. As we continue to think and re-think that life is difficult, or life is unfair, we keep adding to the pain. Remember what Mayo Angelou told Oprah, "When you know better, you do better." When we know we can change things, but we choose not to, it is like the girl at Mike's work. We sit and bang our heads, and then we wonder why it hurts.

For sixteen years, every November 12th, I got sad and depressed. My Dad died on Saturday, November 12, 1994. This year when the anniversary of his death rolled around I wasn't sad or depressed. In fact I was happy and I felt a joy inside when thinking about Dad. I spent more time consciously thinking about my dad's life and the memories I cherish, instead of thinking about his death. *When you know better, you do better*.

I liked not making myself sick and sad this year on the anniversary of Dad's death. It made me feel light and airy. I could feel His love because I had a grateful heart instead of feeling like I had a hole in my heart.

I will say if your grief is new, or if you have no idea what I am talking about when I say things like conscious thinking, mindfulness, awake, or thinking on purpose, then go ahead and cry. In fact, you need to cry and process through the stages of grief shared earlier by Dr. Elizabeth Kübler-Ross. When you reach the place where you want to make a change, remember, the choice is yours. It is only a matter of changing your thought flow, or re-programming your brain.

The Big Iron

Our brain is to our being what a central processing unit (CPU) is to a computer. The CPU and the human brain both carry out the instructions given. I remember when Sheila and I met at Opryland USA. The theme park's computers were driven off of the mainframe. There was a building that stood behind The Nashville Network (TNN) building. The only purpose for this building was to house the mainframe computer for all things Opryland. A whole building! I laugh today knowing my iPhone has more processing power than that old CPU at Opryland.

A computer comes with a CPU and hardware only. Until a software program is installed, the computer can't compute. I remember buying my first computer and being so disappointed when it wouldn't do anything. I called our computer tech friend Brian and asked him to come over and tell me what was wrong with my brand new computer. When he looked at it he laughed, and said, "You goof, you don't have any software installed. It doesn't have anything to do." Computers can't think. They have to be programmed in order to do what we want them to do. The computer's thinker is called a programmer. A programmer designs software to instruct the CPU. The CPU crunches the incoming data and presto. The results are exactly what were programmed. We are "the same but different." Just as computer technology has advanced tremendously the past 25 years, so has the field of neuroscience and brain research.

The principles and laws of the universe have not changed, but the knowledge and popularity of thinking on purpose, awareness and optimism have advanced. Choosing to think in new ways has turned my life from good to great. With every thought I look for the good in everything. During a break at the murder trial of the man who killed Marcia Trimble, I talked to a lady named Teresa who worked for the DA's office. She told me about a program her husband was a part of at the University of Pennsylvania.

The Master of Applied Positive Psychology (MAPP) program was established under the leadership of Martin E.P. "Marty" Seligman in 2003. MAPP is the first educational initiative of the Positive Psychology Center. I do not personally know this man, but I love what he is doing. There are big changes coming. After hundreds of years of studying mental illness, experts are finally investigating and attempting to measure mental wellness. Universities are beginning to teach how to have the good life.

THiNKING CONSCIOUSLY ROCKS!

I know everything in life that happens isn't going to make us happy, but it doesn't have to steal our joy either. Sometimes I have to slow myself down and pretend I am back in Honduras where time stands still. I have to remind myself to be present. Being in the presence of now allows me to see things differently. When I show up and make the most of my day, I see the good in people. When I am sitting at a traffic light, instead of getting anxious I take a moment to breathe and connect with all there is. I use the opportunity of getting nowhere, to relax, reflect, and remind myself to love even this moment in life.

Thich Nhat Hanh is a Vietnamese Buddhist monk who has become an important influence in the development of Western Buddhism. Listening to his audio book titled *Mindfulness and Psychotherapy,* which is excerpts from a week-long retreat, he describes eating a cookie mindfully. When we are not present we miss the great and most simple pleasures of life. Thây, as his friends call him, told a story of when he was a small boy, only four or five years old. His mother would come from the kitchen and give him a cookie. He would eat his cookie in a way that would make it last. He took the cookie outside, in the front yard. He looked at the sky, and the clouds and the leaves— he took a very small bite of the cookie. He was aware if he didn't eat the cookie very slowly it would disappear quickly.

After he took a small bite, he touched the cat with his feet and he touched the leaves, then he took another bite. He said it might take him a half an hour to finish eating his cookie. He was in paradise and in touch with the wonderful things in life. He didn't have much to worry about or regret. He was free to enjoy the cookie. It is this kind of awareness that slows us down and allows us to recognize all there is to be grateful for.

Personally, I need reminding a lot of the time. A few years ago when the idea of this book was coming together and I was developing a practice of mindfulness, the idea that *Thinking Rocks* came to me. I am sure it stemmed from the Nike "swoosh" rock. Carrying that rock in my pocket made me think just do it. Whatever I wanted to do, I tried it. I didn't let anything stop me from moving forward. After a while I started carrying rocks I had written on. The first one I made was think peace. Written with a black marker on a smooth rock, I carried peace in my pocket. Thinking peace eventually moved from my pocket, to my mind and by re-programming my mind to think peace, it moved to my heart. Forgiveness came, love came, joy came, and understanding flooded in with a lot more questions following. *Can it be this easy? Can I really think peace and create inner peace?*

The answer is yes. It really is that easy, but it is not a simple thing to do. Because of our own conditioning, our ego gets in the way sometimes and we make things way more difficult than they have to be. It takes time. We didn't become Small-minded people over night, so we cannot expect to think with a Big-Mind all of the time.

Sheila and I buy houses for pennies on the dollar. We create a budget, a construction plan and hire a contractor to renovate the house to either add to our rental portfolio or to list the house for sale on the Multiple Listing Service. We get to decide ahead of time what we want that house to look like when the project is finished. The outcome begins with our vision of what we want the house and deal to look like, from design, to how much money we make in the end. Some deals go as planned and others change during the process. Sometimes we run into codes issues or more repairs are needed than were budgeted for.

Depending on the market, the house may take longer to sell or rent, adding to our holding costs. Sometimes they go more quickly than we expect. We have learned that as long as we give our best, do our best, it always works out for the best.

We need reminding of this occasionally when a project is challenging. We have to tell ourselves it may not be according to plan, but we know we are doing our best and we can live with the results. This is the first time in my life I have been in such a place. I can let go of frustration. I remind myself of the JBT 90 second rule. I ask myself, "How long do I want to feel frustrated?" It doesn't take long before I realize I am the one, not others who is making me feel frustrated.

Keywords

One day the words, gratitude, peace, love, and vision came to me. I didn't know why, but I made rocks with these words written on them. With smooth rocks I found in a creek bed, I wrote on each the words: THiNK gratitude, THiNK peace, THiNK love, and THiNK vision.

I began to carry them with me as everyday reminders. As I began to re-program my brain, my life was being filled with these four ideals. I began to feel grateful for everything, even problems, because I learned so much through the process of resolving them. I felt peace. I had a peace about Carl, no longer feeling rage and anger, sadness or depression. I was filled with gratitude for having known him. I remembered that we shared a lot of great years. I let go of the pain and replaced it with wonderful memories of our times together. I felt a peace about personal finances that allowed me to quit worrying about money. Amazingly the less I worried about money, the more money found its way to me. The more I would THiNK love, the more I was able to see people just as they are and love them, without wanting to change something about them. My heart was filled with love for the man who murdered my brother. I realized we are all one and what I do to another, I do to myself.

If I love myself; how could I not love someone else? As I became more conscious and aware of all things, a grateful heart emerged. I continually felt myself moving from a Small-Mind to a Big-Mind. As I began to awaken and harness the power within, not a week went by that I didn't have what Oprah calls, an aha-moment. What is really cool is they continue to happen. As I challenged conventional thinking, a path was set before me. Where it will lead, I can only imagine but I am so thankful for where it has brought me so far.

"Our deepest fear is not that we are inadequate. Our deepest fear is that we are powerful beyond measure. It is our light, not our darkness that most frightens

us. We ask ourselves, who am I to be brilliant, gorgeous, talented, and fabulous? Actually, who are you not to be? You are a child of God. You're playing small doesn't serve the world. There is nothing enlightened about shrinking so that other people won't feel insecure around you. We were born to make manifest the glory of God that is within us. It is not just in some of us: it's in everyone. And when we let our own light shine, we unconsciously give other people permission to do the same. As we are liberated from our own fear, our presence automatically liberates others."

~ Marianne Williamson

Chapter 11

Dreaming Awake—Vision

"Our truest self is when we are in dreams awake."

~ Thoreau

"If one advances confidently in the direction of his dreams, and endeavors to live the life which he has imagined, he will meet with success unexpected in common hours."

~ Henry David Thoreau
(1817-1862) Author and Transcendentalist

Mounted to a wall in my bathroom is a 7x magnification mirror. It is positioned perfectly for our height. Sheila and I bought the mirror to show what needs tweezing and to help with applying makeup. Recently it has become more useful to me in another way. Any time these days I think someone or something is stupid, I have to go into my bathroom and look at what stupidity looks like. Do you know what seven time's stupid looks like? It is difficult to look because I am the stupid one when I allow myself to judge another person.

I know I am a better person when I look for the good in everyone and everything. I know things are not as they appear. I know I can be Mindful and unconditionally loving, but I also know I am human and sometimes I do and say stupid things.

When I think, feel or question someone else's actions, motives, beliefs or words because I don't like it or don't agree with it, I am outside of my business. It is stupid for me to want or expect them to do anything other than what they do. Fortunately every time I look in the stupid mirror I see that judging mind looking back at me. If I spend enough time at the mirror, slowly but surely, understanding creeps in, acceptance makes an appearance, and my true self emerges.

The judging mind is replaced with love, unconditionally. No questions asked no need for things to be different. I am not saying we cannot want things to be different. What I am saying is that we cannot want things to be different for other people. If we want things to be different in our life, we can make that happen. It is easier than we might think, as long as what we want isn't something we think will bring us happiness. It doesn't work that way. You have heard it a hundred times, *"happiness isn't out there, it comes from inside."* We can have whatever we want as long as what we want doesn't define our happiness.

I am a huge fan of goal setting and dreaming big. It took me a long time to learn what I wanted. What I always tried to get, is what kept me from getting all that I wanted. Sounds crazy right? Imagine you have just jammied-up, brushed your teeth, washed your face, and are diving into bed. You lay there thinking, "I want to have an awesome dream tonight." I don't know anyone who lies down and before going to sleep, thinks, "I hope I have a nightmare.

Ask yourself these questions: What if our life is nothing but a dream? What would you make it out to be, awesome or nightmarish? What if, what I think about during the day manifests what is in my life? What would I think about?

Sheila and I often ask people, "If you could be anything, do anything, go anywhere, who would you be, what would you do and where would you go?" You may not know the answers to the question. It's okay—you have never given yourself the opportunity to think about such things. If you don't know the answers—let me ask this, "If you did know what you would do? Who would you be? Where would you go?"

Power of Visualization

Before the actor/comedian Jim Carrey was ever famous he learned the power of visualization and practiced it in his life. Here is an excerpt from an interview of Jim Carrey that aired on February 17, 1997 on Oprah:

Oprah: "When you were broke and poor, you used to go up on Mulholland Drive and park and visualize seeing yourself as…"

Carrey: "Yeah that's right. Yes I would visualize having directors interested in me and people that I respected, saying 'I like your work.' I would visualize things coming to me that I wanted."

Oprah: "Was this around 1987, 1985?"

Carrey: "Yes, this was at a time I had nothing, but it made me feel better. I would drive home thinking, *but I do have these things, they're out there, I just don't have a hold of them yet.*"

Oprah: "So you would get this from self-help books, or whatever?"

Carrey: "Yes, the self-help section and they have re-named it the Jim Carrey Wing."

Oprah: "So didn't you write yourself a check? I heard that you did, is that true?"

Carrey: "Yeah, I wrote myself a check for $10,000,000 for acting services rendered and I gave myself five years, three years maybe, and I dated it Thanksgiving 1995. I put it in my wallet and it deteriorated and deteriorated, but then just before Thanksgiving 1995 I found out I was going to make $10 million dollars on, Dumb and Dumber I think it was."

Oprah: "So you visualized yourself like…"

Carrey: "Yeah, yeah."

Oprah: "Visualization works if you work hard."

Carrey: "Yeah, well yeah that's the thing; you can't just visualize and then go eat a sandwich."

My first introduction to the Law of Attraction came from reading a book my friend John Hickman told me about. *The Secret* by Rhonda Byrne is a message of hope. We really can live the life of our dreams. Byrne states people create their own reality and thoughts are things. The secret is the law of attraction and it is always operating. You attract into your life what you think about most. For this reason when we think small-minded, the world is very small and our life is a struggle. We are critical and judgmental and life never seems just right. When we think with a big-mind, life is much easier. Unconditional love flows and we have inner peace, our life is exactly what it is supposed to be and we find happiness. It is our choice to live however we chose.

Many years passed after my brother was murdered before I learned how to apply the law of attraction in my own life. Inner peace didn't come instantly. It took a while for my brain to wrap around the idea that my thoughts cause my feelings and as long as I continued to think bad thoughts, I felt bad. When I was able to change my thoughts to good thoughts, I felt good.

Wayne Dyer says, "There are only two emotions—fear and love, go with love." For too long I went with fear. Maybe I was afraid to let go of Carl or the memory of him. I'm not really sure why I chose to hang onto such unpleasant thoughts. I guess I didn't know better. But I know now and when we know better, we do better. When we do better, we get better. We get to BE happy right here where we are, growing each and every day.

Designing Your Life (DYL)

One way to get from no excitement each morning when you get up, to living a life you actually enjoy, is to visualize your dream life. I created a vision board. (More on that later) Before I could create a vision board, I had to know what excited me about life. I asked myself, what are my dreams, my goals, and my passions? What makes me excited? What do I want out of life? We live in a world, especially in the U.S., of mentally bankrupt thinkers. We know what we don't want but not what we want.

The following is a simple exercise, but don't underestimate its power. Notice I didn't say it is easy, but simple. The simple part is writing the list, the hard part is clearing your head long enough for the creativity to flow. Make a list of all the things you want in your life—the things that get you excited. Once you allow yourself some time and space, the thoughts will come. Only you know the desires of your heart. You know your likes and dislikes, your joys and fears. Allowing yourself the freedom to dream allows your thoughts to shift to things that excite you. Until you know what excites you, it is difficult to know what to add to your vision board.

If time and money were no problem, who would you be? Where would you go? What would you do? Who would you help? If failure was not an option—what would your life look like? We have to loosen the bind and become a conscious thinker, allowing ourselves to dial (DYL) into the universe and place an order for our purposefully-designed life.

Sheila and I love to sail. When we are out on the lake we can adjust the sails and set a course or we can allow the wind to take us. We are either the skipper of the vessel, controlling where it goes, or it goes wherever the winds blow us. The same goes for life; we set our direction by designing each day— designing your life (DYL), instead of allowing life to dish out what it may.

Dream Awake

When we dream it is our subconscious mind at work. I want you to dream awake, using your conscious mind. In the spaces below, dial into the universe and DYL by creating your want list. Think big, dream bigger! The more descriptive you can be the better.

You may notice at first that things you don't want will pop into your mind. You might think, "I don't want this car anymore," or "I don't want to commute 50 miles to work, to a job I hate." Changing those thoughts to the positive may look like, "I want a new car; a silver Infinity fx35 with leather interior and a built in GPS, and luggage racks on top, or I want to work from home, doing meaningful work, generating a six-figure income, encouraging people to live the lives of their dreams." Doing this exercise may sound and feel self-serving, but choosing not to do it keeps your dreams locked in your subconscious.

Creating a vision board makes your dreams come to life. DYL moves you into the action mode and you get to be the director of your life. Otherwise your life is like our sailboat, just being blown around by the wind.

Once you take action by DYL, things start to happen. Life takes another course. You have changed your direction and the laws of the universe will take over and bring the things into your life that you have ordered—sometimes better. Don't feel selfish doing this exercise. You can and will help other people once you are in control of your destiny. You first have to get your life under control and then you really help others.

Your list can contain both material possessions and states of being like happiness and inner peace. If love is what you are looking for, visualize the perfect mate. Write down what this person looks like. Begin to live your life as if they have already come into your life. Make room for their clothes in your closet.

If more money is what you want, imagine getting a raise or a new job. Be creative, you may be the inventor of the next hottest gadget that will make you millions. You never know where the money may come from. You just have to believe that it is on its way. Dream awake.

DYL List: Start with ten things and add more as you like.

1.
2.
3.
4.
5.
6.
7.
8.
9.
10.

THiNK Vision by Creating a Vision Board

As children we get to imagine and pretend and no one think anything of it. For some reason, as we age we lose that imagination. We grow into adulthood and get jobs and families and one day we wake up and ask, "Who am I?" We are living lives not recognizing who we really are. We might ask, "How did I wind up doing what I am doing?" I love using sailing as a metaphor for life. Nearly every time I'm on the lake, something comes up about sailing that I can relate to living truthfully.

Remember, to get anywhere you have to have a heading, set your course. At this point in your life a vision board can be your heading.

After having completed your DYL list, you now have ten things you want in life. Use those ten things and begin to create your vision board.

What is a Vision Board?

A vision board (also known as a creativity collage, a treasure map, or a visual explorer) is nothing more than a board of some type, (I use a cork board, but poster boards are the most popular.), on which you glue, paste, or stick images. You can find these images in magazines, newspapers or on the internet.

The reason I am asking you to THiNK Vision by creating a vision board is because when you surround yourself with images of what you want your life to look like, your life will start to mimic those images.

For instance, before I ever started writing this book, I designed the cover of the book. I printed it out and stuck it on my cork vision board hanging over my desk. I had to see it, know what it was going to look like. I had to THiNK about it before I could ever draw it into my life. The cover has gone through many revisions before it wound up like it is now. But still it was in front of me, I could see it, and it became real to me. The more I thought about it, the more real it became. I know this is not the only factor in bringing this book to life. I couldn't just pin the cover on my vision board and expect it to happen. I had to do something about it. I got up at 4:00 a.m. many mornings to write. I took action and doors started to open.

Editors, publishing, marketing, and such followed. Taking the time to design the cover and visualize what I wanted made this book indelible in my mind. Not everyone who creates a vision board does it the same way. There are many ways for creating your vision board; they are all the same but different; but they serve the same purpose. I am sharing several methods for you to choose from. Depending on where you find yourself on the path to designing your life, you may wish to create your own method. By all means, feel free. It is your VISION; make it whatever you want.

Taking the list you made earlier of the things you want in life, and adding these supplies, you can Design Your Life to be whatever you want it to be. Here is what you will need.

Supplies to Create a Vision Board

- Want list
- A poster board or cork board
- Newspapers, magazines or pictures printed from the internet
- Scissors
- Glue, tape, a stapler, or push pins (It really depends on how fancy you want to go.)

Six Steps to Creating Your Vision Board

1. Create your "want list.'

2. Cut pictures from magazines, newspapers or from the internet. Allow yourself to think big and dream bigger. Have fun with it, cut pictures or headlines that move you. If it gives you a great feeling inside cut it out. Gather a bunch of pictures, images of all kinds; banners, headlines or simply one-word headings.

3. Go through the stack of clippings and select your favorites.

4. Lay them out on your board. Let your creative side (yes, we all have one) take over and trust it to choose the images, and their placement on your board. You may decide to label each corner of your board for different things in your life (Mind, body and spirit, or health, vocation, travel, relationships, spirituality, education, personal development, or family and friends). Maybe your board looks like a collage with images all over the place. It is your board; make it work for you.

5. Apply the images to your board.

6. Add a picture of yourself somewhere on your vision board. It is about your life and you need to show up in the very center of it.

7. Hang your vision board in a place where you will see it every day.

My Vision Board

I already mentioned this book was on my vision board. I'd like to share a few other things that I envisioned that have come to pass. When I first created a vision board I pinned up a picture of a sailboat. Neither Sheila nor I knew how to sail at the time, but within two years we learned how to sail. We joined a local yacht club and we now have the pleasure of sailing any of four club boats. We planned on buying a sailboat after we learned how to sail, but this deal was even better. We pay an annual membership fee; instead of paying a slip fee, boat insurance, maintenance, the cost of a boat and any other expense of owning our own boat. The club is called Percy Priest Yacht Club, but don't let the word yacht make you think this is some ritzy club. The people are great, friendly, and very down to earth and they love to sail. This isn't some snobby group and the fees are extremely reasonable.

Sheila and I pay about $500 a year and we get our choice to sail either one of two Catalina 22s, an O'Day 23, or a smaller O'Day 17. When we take one more class we can sail the club's Norstar 24 inboard-motor sailboat. Pinning the sailboat to our vision boards allowed us to see this dream and draw it into reality.

Sheila has a vision board over her desk as well, and though many of our dreams are the same, some are individual dreams. One of The Seeds of Peace cards that I gave away at *A Season to Remember* has been pinned to my vision board for years. I have no doubt by consciously thinking peace, (and through grace), peace came to me—the peace that passes all understanding. I can't even explain how I feel today about Carl other than saying when I think of him I am filled with joy and not sadness. The same goes for his murderer; I do not hate this man. I feel a love for him that is unexplainable.

Pinned to my vision board are pictures of tiny houses, they look like the green houses from a Monopoly game. There are fifty houses because that is how many rental properties Sheila and I wanted to own when we started investing in real estate. We thought if they would all cash flow $200 each, we could make $10,000 a month from our rentals. Today we own 74 rental properties. They are not all in our company. We own 48 in our company and twenty-six in two other partnerships.

Did we get here by pinning houses to a vision board? Yes and no. Yes, because we got clear on what we wanted and we took the action to make it happen. No, because it takes more than pinning a picture to a corkboard. Jim Carrey said it best when he said, "You can't just visualize it and then go eat a sandwich."

Sheila and I both love to travel, so we pinned our passport to our vision board. The year after we did this, we went on three cruises and two other trips. We were not big travelers until we visualized ourselves being able to travel. Instead of saying things like, "we can't afford to go on that trip," we now say, "How can we make it happen?" Be careful what you say, your words are powerful. Henry Ford said, "if you think you can or can't, you're right."

The reason I asked you to be specific when making out your "I Want" list is because I too wrote myself a check. Just like Jim Carrey, but not for $10 million, (not yet). Each December we start setting our goals for the upcoming year. In 2007, I wrote a check payable to Connie Williams and or Sheila Tidwell for $250,000, payable December 31, 2008. What I meant was we would actually make an income of $250,000, but what we got was $237,236.39 of rental income. With income comes expenses—we didn't really make $250,000. Although I am not complaining, that is a whole lot of rent money.

Being specific will define your wants more clearly to you and to the universe. The way I wrote the check and what I said when I wrote it was, "I want to make $250,000" and I guess we technically did, if we include the income we made from renovating and selling houses. I learned I had to be more specific with an end goal in mind, a net amount. In making a plan for the net amount, Sheila and I take the total dollar amount we want to make and break it down into categories of what we do: rental properties, rehabbing properties, selling properties on the MLS, and selling promotional products. We realized in order to make the money we wanted; we had to develop other streams of income. In the last 3 years we have taken three streams of income and turned it into seven streams of income. Rental, rehab, promotional goods, consulting/coaching, podcast monetization, REALTOR® commissions, and the seventh stream will come from book sales, speaking and seminars.

We used to think it is hard to make more money. For me, the money didn't start to come in until I let go of the need for more. The day I heard the message—*what is it with you and money? How much do you need? What are you going to do with all of it when you get it?* was the day my thinking changed about money. For all of my life I knew I wanted to be rich. What I had never thought of is why. I never asked myself why! I mean the kind of why asking like a kid does. Why, why, why? Here is the way the conversation finally went, when I did sit down and ask why.

Why do I want to be rich? *So I can have money.*

Money for what? *For whatever I need.*

Why do you need more money to buy what you need? *When you say it that way, I do have what I need. I just want more money to buy what I want then.*

What is it about what you want that makes you want whatever that is? *If I have enough money to buy whatever I want, I can be happy knowing I can buy whatever I want.*

Can't you be happy now? *I am happy now most of the time, but if I had.....wait a minute. I am happy now. All of my needs are met. I have food, shelter, and clothing. I needn't anything more. I am such a goof for thinking things that I can buy can somehow make me happier. God, I am so thankful for what I have. I really don't need to make more money to be happy. I don't need a bigger house or a new car to be happy. I can be happy now.*

When I understood it was the wanting and the grasping for more that kept me from being totally happy, it was very easy to loosen the grasp for more and drop the wanting. I suddenly felt a peace about money, and having no money worries was a wonderful place to be.

When I understood that living in the now meant that all of my needs are met, I found myself weeping because the need for more money was gone.

Do I have millions sitting in the bank? Not yet. But knowing I can live peacefully, without grasping for more is the very reason more and more money is coming into my life. My vision for this book is to travel, sharing the message that *Thinking Consciously Rocks*, speaking to hundreds if not thousands of people at a time. I want people to know when we loosen our grasp on the wanting for things, all the things we need come easily to us. We slowly awaken to the purpose of life, one conscious thought at a time. The purpose of life is to live our best life, be happy, and share our talents with others.

Don't live in that quiet desperation Thoreau wrote about, dream awake and create the life you want to live

Chapter 12

Think Gratitude, Peace, Love & Think Vision

"Faith moves mountains, if faith were easy there would be no mountains." ~ Immacelee Ilibagiza

"Our power is in our ability to decide."

~ Richard Buckminster Fuller (1895-1983)
20th century U.S. architect, engineer

"The love of a single heart can make a world of difference." Immaculee Ilibagiza wrote this in her book *Left to Tell: Discovering God Amidst the Rwandan Holocaust.* My heart ached for her when I read her book several years ago. *Left to Tell* recounts her days during the 1994 Rwandan genocide. For ninety-one days Immaculee Ilibagiza hid in a small hidden bathroom with seven other women. The genocide claimed nearly all of her family, only one brother survived. An estimated 800,000 people died in approximately 100 days during the mass murder.

Visualization is seeing our hearts' desire and it sends the

energy of positive thinking to work in the universe. That's what Immaculee did while hiding from machete wielding Hutu warriors. Through God's grace and her actions, she was left to tell. She tells of visualizing French soldiers that will come and rescue them. The women were eventually rescued by French soldiers just as she saw in her mind's eye. What a magnificent story she shares. A story that made me grateful for having lost only one brother and one parent that same year that was designated as the International Year of the Family. We think our problems are too much to handle, until we hear the story of another.

Gratitude, peace, love, and vision were four things I wanted to focus more of my attention on. To help me focus my attention I created product called THiNKING Rocks. I met with a local importer who has manufacturing contacts in China and placed an order for the rocks. They are small die-cast pieces of zinc with the word THiNK followed by one of the four keywords: gratitude, peace, love, and vision. I would never have imagined how carrying a rock with me could become a catalyst for my life, but it did.

Focusing our thoughts on what we want draws those things to us. Do you want inner peace? You cannot have inner peace and think miserably, you have to THiNK peace. Each day carrying a rock with me served as a reminder to monitor my thinking. Bringing to mind whatever word was on the rock.

At first I carried a THiNK gratitude rock in my pocket. I don't recall how long I carried this rock before I realized I truly felt grateful for all things in my life. That included challenges, because I learned that challenges are opportunities to learn and grow. When I felt I could say I was truly grateful for all things in my life, I started carrying THiNK peace. When unhappiness or discontent was present, I had to remember to THiNK peace. As I began to understand more about how to maintain inner peace, I started carrying the THiNK love rock. Having   this rock in my pocket reminded me that we are all one—of the same energy. What I do to one, I do to all. It is amazing how a simple chunk of zinc in my pocket is enough to make me check my thoughts, but it does. The rock I have been carrying for the last year is THiNK vision. It reminds me to take time each day to meditate and calm my mind. Meditation has brought more clarity into my life. Visualizing my life makes me feel more a part of the big picture. Knowing I have a heading and have set my sails for the course, I know the direction in which I am headed. I may not have a choice how each day turns out, but instead of trying to change the wind, I adjust my sails.

These rocks remind me to pay attention to my intention. *THiNKing CONSCIOUSLY ROCKS!* is the title of this book because I believe thinking consciously rocks, and I also know that carrying something to remind me of that helps me every day.

p.e.ACE

The Cumberland River crested just below fifty-two feet in Nashville, a level not seen since 1937. Two-day rain totals in some areas were greater than nineteen inches. The May 2010 Tennessee floods were 1000-year floods and for days afterwards affected many areas and thousands of people. Lives were lost and there was widespread property damage, leaving many people displaced and homeless.

Sheila and I had nine properties affected but didn't lose much in comparison to those who lost their lives or their homes. We gained many things from the flood and one was a screech owl. He made the half a mile flight from the river to a tree in our back yard. I wasn't able to get a good picture of him the first night, but when he returned the second night I was ready. Equipped with my forty-fifth birthday present from Sheila, the

Canon 50D captured a picture I'm sure *National Geographic* would print. We never had an owl in our yard before. We talked to him as he sat in the tree. He stayed two nights and never returned.

Several weeks later Sheila spent Memorial Day at her parent's house and I stayed home to write. There weren't many words written that day, but instead the birth of p.e.ACE. Who is Ace you might ask? He is an animated version of the owl that came to visit us after the floods. For some reason instead of writing that day I thought *Thinking Rocks* (the rocks, not the book) needed a logo. I have always admired the Jacob Brothers for starting their company, *Life is Good*®. This company consistently promotes an optimistic outlook and healthy messages through fun designs and simple words of wit and wisdom. My goal is to create a novelty line using "Ace" as the face of *Thinking Rocks*®; much like *Life is Good*® and their logo Jake.

I never had an imaginary friend growing up, but as an adult I imagine Ace sitting on my shoulder and as long as I am at peace, he stays. The moment I lose my temper, judge another or think with a Small-Mind, he flies away. Once I think with a Big-Mind again and feel inner peace return, in flies Ace. I think the world needs more optimism and for that to happen, we all have to think optimistically.

Advisors and Mentors—who makes you think?

Writing this book has been the most interesting journey of my life. I have learned so much in the process. I have heard personal finance coach and radio host Dave Ramsey, say "Don't take financial advice from broke people." As I wrote this book I realized why I had to *quit telling people what to do.* My goal was to share a message of joy and hope with others, but I had to find inner peace before I could share that hope with others.

I have reached a place where grief no longer controls my life. Not even the anniversary day of a loved one's death can steal my joy. I have discovered there is no way to happiness; rather happiness is the way. Thank you to Dr. Jill Botle Taylor for sharing your *insight* and letting us know we do have a choice about how to respond to life. I love knowing I am the programmer of my brain and can consciously decide to do the right thing. Thank you, Byron Katie for sharing *Loving What Is* with the world.

Understanding reality is "what is this moment," and wanting anything different than *what is* causes suffering and pain. Eckhart Tolle, had it not been for you, my thoughts would be in the past or future, instead of here and now. Thank you for sharing the *Power of Now* with us.

Making this world a better place is a job for all of us and it can only be done through changing the way we think. God is a powerful energy that runs through us all. The world, no, the universe and all that is in it shares this energy. When we tap into the conscious knowledge, we allow ourselves to be whatever we aspire to be.

Thomas Merton, the Trappist monk and author said, "Stop thinking of God as 'a being', but just being." The same is true for us. Life isn't about being rich, being married, or being in love. It isn't about being happy, sad, or successful—life is about being.

I came to understand when I sat with a dying friend; the most help I could be was to be present. When we are in the presence of death it is like the gates of the two worlds open. Neighbor Jay taught me that day what matters in the end is that we love well. Being present for the dying taught me how to be present for the living. Being here and present every day allows me to reach my authentic self. I feel good about myself, and that helps me feel good about life.

When we own our thoughts, dreams, desires, and actions—nothing can stand in our way of creating a phenomenal life. This is what can make a difference in all of our lives—and in so doing we make the world a better place.

I want to close this chapter, this book with three questions and three comments. Before I do, please accept my deepest gratitude for allowing me to share this story. Writing this book has been one of my greatest accomplishments and I am honored you took the time to read it. Thank you! I would like to return the favor one day, and read your book.

The New York Times reported, "According to a recent survey, 81 percent of people feel they have a book in them...and should write it." The sad thing is very few people will act on that feeling. You can do it! Your life matters and I want to hear your story. May peace be with you—always.

Questions:

1. Why do you think the thoughts you think, and believe what you believe?
2. Do your thoughts unite or divide, resulting in conditional or unconditional love?
3. What do you do to be present, kind, and loving?

Comments:

1. You are unique; one of a kind and the world needs you to be your best.
2. You are unique. You have strengths and talents no one else has.

3.You are unique, an individual in form, and part of the whole. We are all one.

Decide to use your power, and think consciously.

Epilogue

Living Fully

THiNKING CONSCIOUSLY ROCKS! was born from a journey to the deepest part of my soul. The journey continues and will continue until the day I take my last breath. The sixteen months following the genesis of this book was truly life changing. I questioned my beliefs. My brain was stretched and my relationships were tried and tested. My ego was inflated at times, and other times my spirit rose and gently deflated my huge ego in such a way that love always emerged.

Love is what always brought me back to balance. When times get scary, when things seem out of control they usually are. It is always our ego and never our spirit that gets us into trouble. My ego wants to tell you how to love; my spirit just wants to show you love. My ego wants to tell you how to laugh or when or what to laugh at, my spirit just laughs. My ego wants to tell you how to live; my spirit says *live and let live*.

I am grateful for the opportunity to love, laugh and live in this moment, right now, because right now is forever.

May we always choose to love, laugh, and live in the now.

Cheers!

Connie Williams

Description of Young Lady/Old Lady

The young lady is looking over her right shoulder, while the old woman is looking straight ahead with her eyes cast downward. Both women's shoulders are positioned at a 45-degree angle. The white part of the picture at the top right section is a veil on the young lady and a head-scarf on the old lady. The upper solid black area is their hair, forming bangs for the old lady and a side shot of the young lady. The old lady's left eye is the left ear of the young lady. The old lady's nose is the same as the young lady's cheek and jawbone.

"My Wife and My Mother-in-Law," by cartoonist W.E. Hill 1915

Acknowledgement

This book project is complete because of so many people, and it is not possible for me to create a thank you list and name each person who helped. However, there are a few who I would like to acknowledge with deep gratitude.

—Peggy DeKay: A remarkable editor who became a friend in the process.

—Breanna Bell, Steve and DeeDee Brickner, Melissa Crim, and Sher Powers: Thank you for your honesty when I needed it most.

—Mary Elizabeth Williams: Thank you for your undying support, encouragement and many nights of proof reading.

—Scott Couch, Leslye Hernandez, Randy Stephenson, Arden von Haeger, and Ady Zouzounis: Thank you all for being my five readers and sharing your thoughts. Your input was amazing.

—Autumn Ringelstein: Thank you for your enthusiasm about this book.

—Joanne and Dan Miller: Thank you for your friendship.

—Sheila Tidwell: You are my partner in life, best friend, my processer, and advisor. I love you.

About the Author

Connie Williams is a real estate investor, podcaster, speaker, REALTOR®, amateur sailor, and Conscious Thinker™.

An entrepreneur for 20 plus years, she loves working, photography, reading, being at the beach, and colorful sunsets.

It took more than 15 years after the unsolved murder of her brother Carl before she learned forgiveness, peace and happiness, and what she calls the true meaning of life.

Together with her partner, Sheila Tidwell, the two co-host *Connie and Sheila Talk: Real Life, Real Estate, Real Fun.* The weekly podcast is available on iTunes and at www.ConnieandSheilaTalk.com. Connie and Sheila live in Nashville, Tennessee with their two dogs, Blake and Riley. This is her first book.

Bibliography

Ajahn, Brahm, *Mindfulness, Bliss & Beyond,* Wisdom Publications, 2006

Ajahn, Brahm, *Opening the Door of Your Heart,* Bolinda Publishing Pty Ltd, 2009

Allen, James, *As a Man Thinketh,* G. P. Putman's Sons, 1896

Byrne, Rhonda, *The Power of Love,* Atria Books, 2010

Byrne, Rhonda, *The Secret,* Atria Books/Beyond Words, 2006

Covey, Stephen, *The 8th Habit: From Effectiveness to Greatness,* Free Press, 2005

Eastman, P.D., *Are You My Mother?,* Random House, 1960

Haanel, Charles, *The Master Key System,* Psychology Publishing, 1912

Hanh, Thich Nhat, *Mindfulness and Psychotherapy,* Sounds True, Incorporated, 2006

Ilibagiza, Immaculee, *Left to Tell: Discovering God Amidst the Rwandan Holocaust,* Hay House, 2007

Kabat-Zinn, Jon, *Wherever You Go There You Are: Mindfulness Meditation in Everyday Life,* Hyperion, 2005

Katie, Byron, and Mitchell, Stephen, *Loving What Is: Four Questions That Can Change Your Life,* Three Rivers Press, 2000

Kiyosaki, Robert and Lechter, Sharon, *Rich Dad Poor Dad: What the Rich Teach Their Kids About Money That the Poor and Middle Class Do Not!* Warner Business Books, 2000

Kübler-Ross, Elisabeth, M.D., *On Death and Dying*, Macmillan, 1969

Miller, Dan, *48 Days to the Work You Love: An Interactive Study,* Broadman & Holman, 2005

Miller, Dan, *No More Dreaded Mondays: Ignite Your Passion— And Other Revolutionary Ways to Discover Your True Calling at Work,* Crown Business, 2009

Paine, Thomas, *The Age of Reason: Being an Investigation of True and Fabulous Theology,* Printed by Barrois, 1794

Peerman, C. Gordon, D.Min., *Blessed Relief: What Christians Can Learn From Buddhists about Suffering,* Skylight Paths Publishing, 2008

Taylor, Dr. Jill Bolte, *My Stroke of Insight: A Brain Scientist's Personal Journey,* Penguin Group 2009

Tolle, Eckhart, *The Power of Now: A Guide to Spiritual Enlightenment,* Namaste Publishing 1999

Resources

Author's Websites:

Ajahn Brahms's website *Buddhist Monk*
http://www.ajahnbrahm.org/

Dr. Jill Bolte Taylor's website *The Brain Extravaganza*
http://drjilltaylor.com/

Rhonda Byrne's website *Everything Is Possible: Nothing Is Impossible*
http://thesecret.tv/creative-biography.html

Stephen Covey's *Empowering Your Greatness* website
https://www.stephencovey.com/

Immaculée Ilibagiza's website *Immaculée's Messages*
http://www.immaculee.com/

Byron Katie's Blog & website *The Work of Byron Katie®*
http://www.byronkatie.com/
http://www.thework.com/index.php

Robert Kiyosaki's *Rich Dad: Transforming Lives through Financial Education* website
http://www.richdad.com/

Dan Miller's podcast/website 48 Days.com
The Best Way to Predict Your Future Is to Create It

http://www.48days.com/

Dave Ramsey's podcast / website *Take Control of Your Money*
http://www.daveramsey.com/home/

Thich Nhat Hanh's website *Plum Village Meditation Practice Center*
http://www.plumvillage.org/

Gordon Peerman's website *Insight Nashville*
http://www.insightnashville.com/Guides

Eckhart Tolle's website *Creating a New Earth Together*
http://www.eckharttolle.com/

Connie Williams' *THiNKING CONSCIOUSLY ROCKS!*
http://www.ThinkingConsciouslyRocks.com/

Grief Help Websites:

Office for Victims of Crime
http://www.ojp.usdoj.gov/ovc/grants/index.html

Parents of Murdered Children
http://www.pomc.com/

MADD: Mothers against Drunk Driving

http://www.madd.org/

Victim Intervention Program – Nashville, TN

http://www.police.nashville.gov/bureaus/chief/victim_intervention.asp

The Compassionate Friends: Supporting Family after a Child Dies

http://www.compassionatefriends.org/home.aspx

Greif Share: Your Journey from Mourning to Joy

http://www.griefshare.org/

GriefNet.org: Grace Happens

http://www.griefnet.org/index.shtml

Recommended Podcasts:

Connie and Sheila Talk: Real Life, Real Estate, Real Fun

http://www.connieandsheilatalk.com/

Connie and Sheila Talk Online Store

http://www.connieandsheilatalk.com/store/

Dan Miller's podcast and website

The Best Way to Predict Your Future Is To Create It

http://www.48days.com/category/48-days-podcast/

Eckhart Tolle TV: *Creating a New Earth Together*

http://www.eckharttolletv.com/

Joel Osteen Ministries

http://www.joelosteen.com/Broadcast/Pages/Podcast.aspx

Miracle Thought Podcasts by Marianne Williamson

http://www.oprah.com/oprahradio/Marianne-Williamsons-MiracleThought-Podcasts

Morning Coach J.B. Glossinger

http://www.morningcoach.com/

Oprah's Soul Series

http://www.oprah.com/oprahradio/About-Oprahs-Soul-Series-Webcast

Podcast Answerman with Cliff Ravenscraft

http://podcastanswerman.com/

San Francisco Zen Center

http://www.sfzc.org/

Smart Passive Income with Pat Flynn

http://www.smartpassiveincome.com/

Tara Brach: *Meditation, Emotional Healing, Spiritual Awakening*

http://tarabrach.com/audiodharma.html

This American Life

C:\Users\Barbara\Documents\CLIENTS\Connie Williams\Manuscripts\page 205-1.doc

THiNKing Rocks!®

The American motivational speaker, Earl Nightingale said,
"You are what you think about."

THiNK gratitude, love,
peace & vision.
Connie carries one of these rocks
every day as a reminder to
Think Consciously.

Embossed black velvet pouch
with (4) 100% zinc *rocks*

THiNKing Rocks!® Magnets

These mini-billboards remind me to pay attention to my thoughts.

SOMETIMES WE FORGET 2 REMEMBER WHO WE REALLY ARE.

THE OUTER WORLD OF CIRCUMSTANCE SHAPES ITSELF TO THE INNER WORLD OF THOUGHT.

GOOD THOUGHTS; GOOD ACTS. BAD THOUGHTS; BAD ACTS!

CONNECT TO THE POWER THAT CAN CREATE A FLOWER!

BE CALM, BE KIND.

Each magnet is 3″ square / 30 mil thickness. Set of (5)

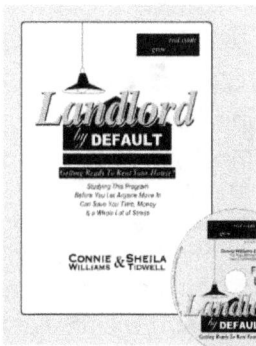

THiNK Real Estate, Grow RiCH

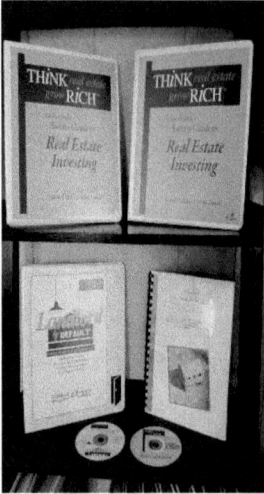

Understand what it takes to be a successful real estate investor and have more knowledge than most landlords. You will know how to find deals and subs, how to manage projects and communicate with subcontractors.

We teach you how to choose a lender either institutional or private, and what to look for in a lender. We will continue to support you in your investing career. We want you to be successful in building your real estate investing business.

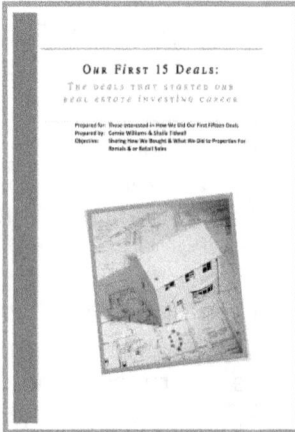

Our First 15 Deals

A start to finish walk-through project with seasoned investors! Here's what you'll learn: How Connie and Sheila found their first 15 deals and financed each of them. You will also learn about the purchase price, rehab budget, and the all-important exit strategy.

All of this and more are packed into a 60 page manual with over two hours of audio.

We invite you to join us each week for our podcast, as we share our newest episode on iTunes and also on our website.

Peace!

Connie & Sheila

www.ingramcontent.com/pod-product-compliance
Lightning Source LLC
LaVergne TN
LVHW051511080426
835509LV00017B/2017